SOUL MAPPING

SOUL MAPPING

An Imaginative Way
to Self-Discovery

Nina H. Frost

Dr. Kenneth C. Ruge

& Dr. Richard W. Shoup

MARLOWE & COMPANY
NEW YORK

Published by
Marlowe & Company,
A Division of the Avalon Publishing Group Incorporated
841 Broadway, 4th Floor
New York, NY 10003

Soul Mapping: *An Imaginative Way to Self-Discovery*

Library of Congress Cataloging-in-Publication Data

Frost, Nina H.
Soul mapping : an imaginative way to self-discovery / by Nina H. Frost,
Kenneth C. Ruge, and Richard W. Shoup
p. cm.
ISBN 1-56924-645-9
1. Self-perception. 2. Self-evaluation. 3. Introspection.
4. Change (Psychology) I. Ruge, Kenneth. II. Shoup, Richard, III. Title.
BF697.5.S43 F76 2000
158—dc21
00-021-893

9 8 7 6 5 4 3

Designed by Pauline Neuwirth, Neuwirth & Associates, Inc.

Distributed by Publishers Group West

Printed in the United States of America

DEDICATION

TO OUR FAMILY AND FRIENDS,
SUSTAINERS ALL

CONTENTS

PREFACE

"Know thyself."

—The oracle at Delphi

WELCOME TO THE ADVENTURE
THAT IS SOUL MAPPING

WHAT IS this book about? Well, it's about *you*. When you are done with this book, you will have a greater sense of your true self than ever before.

Soul Mapping gives you a playful and profound way to capture all the parts of you—past and present—*and* also helps point you toward a future that is authentic, vital and inner directed.

Thanks to this inner-directed process, *Soul Mapping* is a self-help book with a difference—rather than urge you to follow a specific formula or subscribe to the author's views, *Soul Mapping* helps you emerge with a thorough and surprising grasp of who *you* are, who you are becoming, and what parts of yourself you may need to retrieve. The fruits of this book will be different for each reader.

At The Vocare Group, we specialize in helping people discern their calling—the work they are meant to do. As counselors, we work with the psychological aspects of change and transition. As theologians, we are also vitally interested in the spiritual aspects of discovery and renewal. And as workshop leaders, we are always looking for exercises and tools that help people see themselves in new ways and make connections.

Soul Mapping combines our three approaches: the psychological, the spiritual and the practical. We conceived it to elicit epiphanies and reveal connections between the various parts of your life. It's confessional, directional, revealing, and healing. It's also fun. Here's how it works:

PART ONE: CREATING YOUR SOUL MAP

The first part of the book has ten chapters on key themes, each filled with thought-provoking exercises that help you sketch out who you were, who you are, and who you most want to be in terms of that theme. The ten resulting small maps form your large, always revealing Soul Map. The Introduction spells out the process in detail.

PART TWO: LIVING YOUR SOUL MAP

This second part helps you integrate and implement the results of this book's exercises. It looks at fear's role in your life and teaches you how to read your overall map for the spiritual direction it provides.

The poet Rainer Maria Rilke once wrote: "And then comes the knowing that in me there is a space for a second, large, and timeless life." That is the life Soul Mapping speaks to—in all its timelessness, mystery, and sheer singularity. Welcome to the discovery process; welcome to new ways of knowing yourself.

Note: when we, the authors, refer to ourselves in the following text, our names appear in small caps (DICK, NINA, KEN).

INTRODUCTION
"ADMITTING THE ANGELS
KNOCKING AT YOUR DOOR"

———— ❧ ————

"You need to claim the events of your life to make yourself yours. When

you truly possess all you have been and done, which may take some

time, you are fierce with reality."

—Florida Scott-Maxwell, *The Measure of My Days*

THERE'S A reason the most dreaded interview question is "Tell me about your-self." It's the nagging feeling that, despite all the self-help books out there, we just don't know as much as we could about someone so close to home as ourselves.

Soul Mapping is a way to discover different aspects of your true self, elaborate on them, and combine them in a self-description that has integrity and usefulness. Our premise is that our lives constantly present us with clues about how and where we belong. How to capture these hints? We are people with many facets and aspects, some seemingly contradictory. How to integrate and celebrate them?

Soul Mapping is a way to do this capturing and celebrating—to admit what D. H. Lawrence called "the angels who are knocking at our doors." It can also be a way to move on—a way to get your bearings, make changes in your life and move in the direction that is right for you at this time. Soul Mapping can also be about waiting, watching, and listening. It does not exhort you to necessarily change your life; it does give you the type of overview that helps you decide the right action (or inaction) at a given time.

HONORING OUR ROUNDABOUT LIVES

WHEN WE explain our resume to someone or recount our life, we tend to do it in a linear or chronological fashion: First I did this; then I did that. I went to these schools, got these jobs, married or did not marry this person. Moved here, then moved there. And so on. Describing things chronologically helps us and others understand what happened when, but the life you're describing is *lived* in a much more creative, chaotic, radiant way—one that involves many different aspects of your life simultaneously. Soul Mapping is about listening to all those aspects at once, and seeing what they have to say about your past, your present, and your future. It is very much a process of *retrieval*; you gather up the fragments of your-self that may have gotten lost along the way. In doing so, you capture a shifting "big picture."

Soul Mapping honors the path but also the detours; the directions you have taken, but also the sideways glances. It reveals, gently, and invites listening and understanding—the first components of conscious change. By honoring the side-ways glances and inviting them onto the page in a spread-out fashion, this tech-nique frees you from any sense of hierarchy or "better than" aspects of your life. Hopes or ambitions you had as a child are just as important as the ones you have now, as an adult; hobbies and interests are as directive as formal education; and envy is as clue-laden as any longing.

YOU ARE INVITED ON A JOURNEY . . .

SOUL MAPPING is travel in the truest sense of the word. The dictionary defines travel as "to journey through" and also "to associate." Each chapter of Soul Mapping is a "journey through" an evocative topic, seen from the perspective of your past experience, present situation, and future hopes. The technique taps the brainstorming powers of association. In each chapter you become an *explorer*—charting territory familiar and strange; listening for the new and the steadfast; bringing back learnings and resolutions.

How does Soul Mapping help you on this journey? The process weaves together three strands:

1. CAPTURING (AND CONNECTING) DIFFERENT PARTS OF YOU

TEN VERY different chapter themes guide you in generating ten maps that together form one large Soul Map. The themes are deliberately disparate, because we all have shifting and yet ever-present sources of identity and clues as to who we were, who we are and who we most want to be. Often, forgotten or unconscious hints swirl around: childhood, high school or college leanings, friends we envy, detours and frustrations, secret hopes, and wild ambitions. If these topics could be made conscious and visually represented somehow, they could be a source of wholeness and direction.

Soul Mapping does more than evoke past, present and future aspects of our true selves—it puts them on a visual grid and allows you to see the *relationships* between themes—perhaps as never before. You create a psycho-spiritual web of identity that frees you from having to put things in sequence. This process works the way hearing music, seeing a painting or watching a film or a dance does—it's beyond cognition, and has the power to bestow unexpected epiphanies and connections and to help us see ourselves more clearly.

That is the essential premise of Soul Mapping: to bring forth what is within you in a graphic way; to see how these elements link up; to listen to them for the wisdom they hold. That bringing forth is helped by the spirit of exploration, which informs the structure of each mapping chapter.

2. ENGAGING THE SPIRIT OF TRAVEL

ALL PILGRIMAGES have stages, and so does each Soul Mapping chapter. The process invites you, the voyager, to do some thinking and planning about where you are headed (in this case, each chapter's topic). Then you set out, ready to explore; through exercises and reflection you encounter the familiar and the unexpected. You are moved, addressed by surprise. Maybe you even get lost. And you emerge from the destination with new insights, things to remember, promises to act on, and places to revisit.

Like travel, Soul Mapping has the power to change you, to bring you the gift of new sights, discovery and re-discovery: new manifestations of longings, talents and possibilities. When you travel, the whole of a new experience happens in a short, compact, powerful time. Each chapter is designed to be a voyage unto itself, with exercises that take you deep into the topics, using these signposts:

GETTING THE LAY OF THE LAND.

An overview of each topic's importance guides you into it. Why is this topic a part of the whole; why is it important to "visit" it?

BEGINNING EXPLORATIONS: SURVEYING THE PAST AND THE PRESENT.

Exercises and stories will help you form your "first impressions." The real voyaging begins, with explorations into personal history and current feelings.

TRAVELING DEEPER: CHARTING NEW TERRITORY.

Successive exercises widen your experience of the topic, and engage the subconscious. This is a place in the journey for surprise and deep work.

RETURNING: MAPPING WHAT YOU FIND, DREAMING THE FUTURE.

How do you unpack this chapter? How has this chapter spoken to you? What is most pressing? Most surprising? What "angels are knocking"? What discoveries do you want to integrate with the rest of your life?

3. INVOKING THE PAST, PRESENT AND FUTURE

AS THE Soul Mapping process spirals through the stages of exploration, it also weaves together your past, present, and future. As the travel metaphor makes clear, all the stages of exploration present opportunities and have the power to bestow gifts. Similarly, messages from your past, present, and future all need to be heard. The present tells you what's happening and can help you focus on what you are seeking to change. The past is where so much originates. The future is the land of our envisioned changes. Soul Mapping looks at all three. It is a process about *discovery*, whether looking at your past, present or future; and it is a process about *movement*—how to go towards the urgings that filter up in the process of creating your Soul Map.

WE'RE NOT TRAVELING WITHOUT A MAP!

MOST OF us think we are traveling through life without a map. (Or, worse, we are stuck in someone else's idea of our path, all mapped out in unappealing ways.) Many books tap into the spiritual importance of "not knowing"—of relinquishing our "plans." As the old saw reminds: "If you want to make God laugh, outline your plans."

Yet between true and venerable not knowing and following a route not of your own making lies the middle road—a path charted by your Soul Map. Because at any given moment you *do* have internal yearnings, desires, and directions you want to go in. If you stop and take the time to ask, "OK, where am I along these various points in the road?", you will find a map. Not one with a timeline attached, necessarily, detailing where you're going to go and when, but a vivid sense of where you yearn to be. And yearnings can be the first step to something new.

Soul Mapping encourages associations and new paths of thinking. It connects sparks, and links ideas—especially ideas that may have been disconnected from each other. Does a childhood hunch have bearing on what you want to be doing ten years from now? Quite possibly. Is there a connection between who you envy and your own latent talents? That is often the case. Is a neglected desire responsible for the vague sense of unease you're feeling? There's a good chance.

Play with the chapters. Mine them. Some chapters will engage you more than others. Some may make you nervous; some will make you feel free; others, stymied. Try to engage them all, recognizing it is natural to have more energy for some topics and exercises than for others. And realize this is a mysterious process; you don't know which chapter exercise will hold something you need to hear.

A SPACE WIDE ENOUGH TO CALL HOME

BY JUMPING into and simultaneously exploring many different facets of your life, Soul Mapping takes a type of "bird's eye view." It revels in the fact that where your life and future lie can be a place of tremendous *spaciousness*—a both scary and nourishing concept. Soul Mapping taps into the spiritual belief that the world is constantly coming to our door, telling us we are larger than we think we are.

That breadth—that sense of the "wideness" of life—is at the center of Soul Mapping. It's interesting that in Hebrew, the word for "salvation" translates as "broad space." There is something salvific about being in jobs, relationships, or communities that are large enough in spirit, and something diminishing about being in ones that are too small. Soul Mapping counters any sense that we are small, and urges us onto wider playing fields.

Think of the times when you have been in a state of "flow"—utterly present and graceful, moving through space and time naturally and enjoyably. In those times, there is a sense that "all" of you is there. Capturing and celebrating that "all" is very much the Soul Map mission.

WHEN SHOULD I DO A SOUL MAP?

"You know what time it is, how it is now the moment for you to wake

from sleep."

—Romans 13:11

As an awareness tool, a Soul Map invites you to work on it—or a part of it—anytime you want to *wake up* to what your life is saying to you. In this way, any time is the right time to work the process.

There are, however, times when doing a Soul Map can be particularly helpful:

TRADITIONAL TRANSITIONS

A NEW Soul Map is a great companion in times of transition, whether that transition is welcome or otherwise. Transitions like the ones below are all times when the kind of deep listening this work engenders can be nourishing.

- After a divorce or the end of a relationship.
- After a period of ill health.
- Around the time of a graduation, both before and after.

- Before a marriage.
- After a job loss or before a job change.
- After a move.
- After a death.
- During the breakup of a friendship.
- When you need to let go of something or someone.

These outer, manifest types of transitions aren't the only ones aided by this work. Doing a Soul Map can help to *encourage* a wanted transition to happen.

TIMES OF CAREER TRANSITION

THERE ARE many job and career implications to Soul Mapping. Because it is a process that uncovers past and present enthusiasms, it naturally leads to questions of whether the results of your exercises have implications for your work, whether that work is vocational (what you enjoy or feel called to do), avocational (a hobby on the side), or volunteer. This theme of discerning work applications is woven through many of the chapters of this book.

LIMINAL, THRESHOLD TIMES

BESIDES TIMES of clear upheaval or transition, Soul Mapping also beckons during the "in-between" times. Harder to delineate than transitions, but no less important, these are the moments that precede periods of change. They are threshold times, when you know some way of life is ending but the new has yet to fully take shape; when you are working on articulating and defining not just where you're headed, but what's going on. Like the Soul Mapping process itself, these times are not mired in the past; they look toward the future while also open to and aware of the present moment.

These times of impending change blend opportunity with danger. Opportunity to move into something new; danger you will move abruptly or for the wrong reasons. Because Soul Mapping is an inner process—a listening—it can help to keep you from being overly swayed by something outside yourself.

One of the most common "in-between" times is when you are looking for a job. NINA notes the importance of Soul Mapping in her work as a vocational counselor: "For many people, finding work remains a very inadvertent process. You often hear of things from a somewhat haphazard mix of external sources: newspaper or Internet ads that catch your eye, friends of friends, a parent's cousin. These may indeed be great opportunities, but in order to respond to these external possibilities truly and well, you need to have done the inner assessment first, not after you take something to see if you will like it. A completed Soul Map is like an invaluable shield; it proclaims to you (and to interviewers) who you are and what you do well. Just as importantly, it fends off the jobs that simply would not fit."

TIMES YOU NEED NURTURE AND RENEWAL

FOR THE times you are simply tired . . . or down . . . or not feeling connected at all with your creative self . . . or don't even think you *have* a creative self, Soul Mapping can be a way to re-connect with what particularly needs to be cultivated in your life now. A Soul Map is moisture in times of dryness; it "renews" in that it refills your well with a fresh supply of images, symbols, hopes, remembrances, and ideas.

Soul Mapping is in part about helping change and renewal happen, but there's more. We feel there is an "invocation" aspect to this work, too. As a form of deep listening, it is a type of prayer. It asks for things and acknowledges things. Soul Mapping recognizes places where we can move on, and places where we are, in KEN'S words, "constrained by love"—bordered, in part, by sacred familial loyalties and obligations, and required to live and move within them. So it's still worth saying: This is fundamentally mysterious work. And it is honest work. Our goal? To move you toward the "fierce with reality" place this chapter's opening quote speaks of.

DOING A SOUL MAP IN COMMUNITY

BESIDES GIVING thought to when to do a Soul Map, also ponder who you could do it with. While primarily a "self-discovery" tool and activity, Soul Mapping lends itself well to being done in community—whether that community consists of family members, friends, colleagues . . . even perfect strangers.

Indeed, the workshops we run using the Soul Mapping process usually bring people who do not know each other together. They sit at small tables that become communities, brainstorming and creating, partly in introspective silence, partly sharing their fruits and surprises. Something powerful and helpful happens when you speak a section of your map out loud and guide others through what you drew. It is equally illuminating to hear others' stories, see their trajectories, and honor their hopes.

Soul Mapping can also be a valuable tool for spouses and partners wishing to express, share, explore differences, introduce each other (again or initially) to what deeply matters to them.

How to do a Soul Map

SOUL MAPPING asks you to give a visual representation to various parts of your life. There is no right or wrong way to do a map, no one thing it should end up looking "like." We hasten to tell clients that Soul Mapping is not an art contest, and they are visibly relieved.

That said, drawing and colors are key components of the Soul Mapping process. Because this is a way to be playful with the unconscious, and to let things come up, using symbols, objects, colors, stickers, drawings, magazine cut-outs, etc. frees you from relying on words alone to capture what you mean. A lot of the surprise in this process can come from the parts of ourselves that speak in symbol and color. It's the coloring and juxtaposing and drawing that make the material come alive. You go beyond a verbal process limited to words. Themes emerge, freed by color. Symbols come out of pictures. This is a process both conscious *and* spontaneous.

GATHERING YOUR TOOLS: HAVE FUN WITH THE MATERIALS

STEP ONE is to choose whatever art materials you would have fun with. You can do a Soul Map just fine with stick figure drawing, a pen for writing words, and crayons or highlighting pens for coloring, but feel free to break into:

- glitter glue
- feathers
- magazine photos
- pipe cleaners
- popsicle sticks
- stickers

- fuzzy shapes
- wiggly things
- paints

These materials are sold at art and stationery stores and in the kid's crafts sections of toy stores. They can help convey more than words ever can, so it's definitely worth spending some time browsing for a stash of materials you can bring to the table.

PROCESS PRACTICALITIES

1. THE CHAPTER EXERCISES

You start the process with a chapter in Part One, *Creating Your Soul Map*, preferably the chapter called "Capturing Today: Your Here and Now." Then do the rest of the chapters in the order of the book—or whatever order most appeals to you. "Doing" a chapter means traveling through its layers and engaging its various exercises. The chapters have very different exercises; they tackle very different themes. But all chapters will ask you to explore aspects of your past, present and future as you journey through each topic. Many exercises are question-driven, for questions are at the heart of the journey and can open you up to the promptings of the unconscious. Suggestion boxes will appear as signposts to help you along the way.

For each the exercises, take out a big sheet of paper and *brainstorm*: write freely, even wildly. Let first reactions float up. Ponder further. Think in terms of words *and* symbols. Write or draw your responses, depending on what feels right. Try to, in the immortal words of a friend and colleague, "hit the undelete function key in your brain"—that is, let what is ignored, suppressed, rejected, seemingly "too small" or "too inappropriate" to surface. Don't worry about making sense, or contradicting yourself, or what people will think. Just evoke, listen, and capture the data. Tidiness is not the point here.

WELCOMING ALL THAT IS "OUT OF LEFT FIELD"

ESPECIALLY TRY to invoke and make room for the "out of left field" responses that each chapter may bring. Soul Mapping is an inside-out exercise, an open-ended exploration. The chapters are about process, not content. So if something seems strange, or stray, invite it in.

2. TRANSFERRING TO THE CIRCLE PAGE

After you complete each chapter's exercises, you will have a lot of material, some of it a surprise. In their fullness, your chapter exercises remain a source of learning and direction. But it's also useful, after casting a wide net, to *hone*: to take your responses from the exercises and sift them for what is most pertinent, surprising, and vital and then *transfer* those aspects to a place in your map—a page where they can stand out and later link up with the results of other chapters.

The Circle Page summary will be at the end of each chapter's exercises, a series of questions that help you hone in on what is particularly important from the brainstorming and remember what you have just done. The results of these questions—and anything else you want to add from your exercises—are what you put directly on your Circle Page.

3. THE CIRCLE PAGE

You transfer onto your Circle Page the most pertinent contents from your chapter exercises. The circle gives you a sort of sacred container to put in key words; add drawings, color phrases and pictures; glue in small objects; etc.

Feel free to use photo copies of the Circle Page in the back of this book, a larger piece of paper, a larger circle, or no circle at all. We suggest a circle in part because of the great tradition of drawing mandalas: putting shapes, colors and words into a circle is a long-standing way to center oneself in times of transition. Mandalas appear in the religious and artistic traditions of many cultures. Swiss psychologist Carl Jung drew many himself and used them with clients. He felt the mandala provided a protective container to contain the tension of the opposites—a place to order but not ignore all our chaos and contradictions—the very stuff of a Soul Map.

In Soul Mapping, a circle can do two things at once: it invites conflicting parts of our nature to appear in one place, and helps focus concentration by providing a container. Different circles are also easy to arrange into an overall map.

PUTTING IT ALL TOGETHER

EACH CHAPTER stands alone with its Circle Page; combined, the circles become your complete Soul Map. They are the petals of an entire flower; the planets that orbit around the reader who has created them, each an integral part of the whole. On a large piece of paper you assemble the circles in whatever fashion suits you, and can move them around. The contents of each circle emerge as powerful summaries of key aspects of your life. Coloring, moving components, using stickers, etc. make this a visceral, not just an intellectual enterprise.

4. INTERPRETING YOUR MAP

Part Two of the Soul Mapping process, *Living Your Soul Map*, has three chapters that explain how to read your Soul Map for clues, directions, inspiration, and challenges and roadblocks. This section helps you to honor and move with what you see.

EMBRACING YOUR LIFE'S FULLNESS

THE SOUL Mapping process is about pursuing personal integrity in life: how we tap unbounded energy when we do what we love. How we feel when we're in some sort of "flow." Soul Mapping gets you into that flow. It raises your energy level, because rediscovering lost parts of yourself is exciting and vital work.

This book initiates a process of change by awakening the unconscious mind. It starts a journey; shifts what you notice; changes what comes to you. There is a mysterious quality to this work. At its core, Soul Mapping is about being more awake and embracing the fullness of your experience.

Though mysterious, the process traffics in concrete, practical exercises that locate past, present and future energy and authenticity, give it a place on a map and then help you look at how to release what is captive; change what is old; celebrate what is worthy; and listen for what may be faint, but essential.

To "put something on the map" is to make it well known. Soul Mapping is about making you well-known—to you.

Let's begin.

PART ONE

CREATING YOUR SOUL MAP

1

CAPTURING TODAY
Your Here and Now

———— ❧ ————

"Listen to your life. See it for the fathomless mystery that it is. In the

boredom and pain of it no less than in the excitement and gladness:

touch, taste, smell your way to the holy and hidden heart of it because

in the last analysis all moments are key moments and life itself is grace."

—Frederick Buechner, *Listening to Your Life*

Getting the Lay of the Land

Since a lot of the Soul Mapping work is about change and movement and tapping into longings and shifts, establishing where you are *now*—especially the places of possibility or discontent—is essential. The "Capturing Today" chapter is both a check-in point and a departure point.

Though the other chapters of the book can be done in any order that appeals to you, it's a good idea to start any Soul Map with at least a brief look at today, which, needless to say, is always shifting. Though some of the outer "today" components may not shift often—same job, living in same place, etc.—other inner components are always in flux. So this chapter will ask you to look at both the outer and inner elements that make up where you are in the movement of your life now. It will help you take your pulse in ways that can be revealing and help-ful and that position you to do the rest of the chapters. And it will embrace the past, present and future aspects of where you are "today."

STARTING WITH THE BASICS . . . AND TRAVELING DEEPER

IN DREAM analysis, a useful question often is "Who is dreaming this dream?" "Capturing Today" asks, "Who is starting this Soul Map?" Some of the questions and answers will be more factual and descriptive; some will traffic more in subtle shifts and hints of change. All the exercises celebrate the present moment as a crucial place, where past influences and future possibilities meet and converge. As a crucible, the present can be a place of tremendous power and direction . . . and/or confusion and doubt. These exercises can help uncover where your ener-gy wants to lead you.

This chapter is also a good introduction into the spontaneous graphic journal-ing technique that lies at the heart of Soul Mapping. Your off-the-cuff responses will be at the cutting edge of your Soul Mapping data and represent the latest and perhaps the best information and energy. Because of its immediacy, doing the "Capturing Today" chapter just by itself is a valuable technique. You can also do it with a friend, family member, in a group, with a partner, etc. as a way to float up "what's happening" in your lives.

There is a retreat center in upstate New York that uses an exercise where one per-son simply asks the other "What's happening?" over and over. When the person who answers stops talking, the listener repeats the question. It's called the "Fair Witness" exercise and the person listening is supposed to quietly record the unfolding answers in a reverent atmosphere, while the speaker keeps responding in ever-deepening ways. "Capturing Today" is a sort of "Fair Witness" chapter. It asks different ques-tions, but the purpose is to get at various layers simultaneously. Besides being a tech-nique for zeroing in on what's happening, this method honors the sacredness of the present in much the same way as a venerable tradition known as "spiritual direction."

SOUL MAPPING AS SPIRITUAL DIRECTION

A NOTE on the practice of spiritual direction is important here, since Soul Mapping is in part about the same kind of deep listening that spiritual direction works with. Spiritual direction involves discerning how God, the Spirit, etc. may be working in your life. As a practice, it is not limited to any denomination like Presbyterian or Baptist or Catholic. It involves meeting with a qualified director once a month to practice attentiveness; to, as one longtime director puts it, uncover the obvious in our lives and realize that God reaches us through everyday events. Unlike a weekly therapy model which may attempt to understand your past, spiritual direction asks "what is going on *now?*"

Whatever your belief system (if any), this chapter holds up the notion that our present days are times of "continuous annunciation." Each day brings developments, signs and emotions we are meant to notice and listen to for the deeper significance they hold. Like spiritual direction, this part of Soul Mapping focuses on what is happening today; for as the poet Rilke put it, "The encounter with the divine is always *now. . . .*"

Listening to your current life through the process of Soul Mapping then incarnates and makes tangible and accessible aspects of what your soul wants you to hear, and what God may want you to hear. It can be hard to do this kind of listening in daily, chaotic life. The Jesuits developed the tool known as the "Examen"—a sort of profound checklist to ask yourself each night; your answers helped trace the outlines of mysterious, myriad ways God was with you that day. While not a nightly obligation, this chapter of your Soul Map has some of the same ineffable intention. Beyond any dogma or creeds or format, it's about listening.

"LISTENING FOR THE KNOCK"

HOW DO you engage this form of listening, particularly if you are working alone, and not in a spiritual direction relationship? A friend of ours once described going on a retreat as "listening for the knock," and this is a wonderful phrase for Soul Mapping, too.

If "the knock" is the vehicle through which we hear the unexpected, or the hoped for, or whatever our souls need us to hear, it will often come through the ways and means of the Spirit: through surprise, insistence, hunches, imagination, dreams, an inner voice, a nudge, our intuition. In other words, in surprises not engineered by the ego. These are but some of the "angels knocking at your door" that D. H. Lawrence urges us to admit. But it's hard to hear things that are not part of our ego's construct. That's where Soul Mapping comes in. Do the exercises playfully, with open hearts and open minds, and let go of preconceptions and expectations.

ALL THE PARTS OF "TODAY"

AS YOU travel into the territory of this chapter some of the questions may seem to overlap, but remember: There is no right or wrong way to do a Soul Map. The goal is to float up as much information as possible. Some of what you reveal can be incorporated into other chapters.

So grab a notebook, or a stack of paper, and begin. Write and draw as much as you can now; later you can transfer the essence of what you've written to the Circle Page.

BEGINNING EXPLORATIONS:
Surveying the Past and the Present

BASIC SURROUNDINGS

FIRST, TAKE a snapshot of your current circumstances: the people, places and activities that make up your life today.

PEOPLE

- Who are you surrounded by? List family members, friends, co-workers, any others who populate your world. Leave room for additional writing after each name.

NEXT STEP: ELABORATION

What is the current tenor of these relationships? Intimate? Strained? Cordial? Evolving? For each name, jot down whatever adjectives come to mind that characterize the way you currently relate with that person.

- Who do you most love to spend time with? Who are the people who provide exhilaration (and maybe fear) because they really see who you are, enjoy you and challenge you to be your best self?
- On the other hand, who, in the words of writer Anne Lamott, are "people

who make you hold your breath" when you're around them, because they make you uncomfortable and don't let you be who you are?

- Who do you help at this time in your life? Who helps you?
- Write a paragraph describing you at this time in your life from the perspective of a close friend. What would he or she say? (This can be a surprising exercise that is best done quickly, without judging. Writing from another's perspective is freeing and unpredictable; try it and see what comes up.)

PLACE

WHERE ARE you living? What part of the country? What are your surroundings? What type of home are you in—house, apartment, other. How long have you been there?

NEXT STEP: ELABORATION

Do you like where you live? Why or why not? Does where you live feel like "home"—a place of comfort and rootedness? If not, do you have a place that *does* feel like home? Describe why *that* place feels like home.

COMMUNITY

- What communities are you a part of?
  Work-related:
  Social:
  Recreation-oriented:
  Religious:
  Other:

NEXT STEP: ELABORATION

What do these communities mean to you?
Which would you want more of? Less of?
Do you feel controlled by any of your communities?
Have you outgrown any of these communities?
Are there any communities you would like to join?

WORK

- Where are you today in terms of work? Are you employed? Unemployed? If employed, what are you doing, where, what is the scope of your work? If unemployed, what are you looking for, and how would you characterize what you do best? Do you feel under-employed? What parts of you aren't being used?
- What is enjoyable for you to do? What is not?
- What are your "irresistible skills"? The things you can't help but do and enjoy? Does your current job allow for their expression?
- Do you consider yourself adequately valued by your employer? If not, how far off do you feel your perceived value is from your actual value?
- Are you learning in your current job situation? Where are you in the cycle of the life of a job: Just started a new one? Been there a while; know the ropes and enjoying it? Getting bored and ready to move on? Frustrated in a bad work situation? Not ready to move or actively looking?

TRAVELING DEEPER:
Charting New Territory

YOUR ANSWERS to the above questions lay a kind of factual bedrock we will be coming back to. The "facts" you have outlined so far invite deeper exploration:

NAMING THE MASKS

ANY SOUL Map work will bump up against our shifting "personas"—a word that means literally the "masks" or roles we wear in various parts of our life. As natural and necessary as clothing, personas are not harmful per se, as long as we know they are not the whole story. But in any given snapshot of "today," some roles predominate over others. It's good to name these roles and bring them to awareness, because as you discover things you would like to shift in your life, that desire may run into resistance from a persona. Learning they are indeed not the whole story, and that some are outgrown, helps make room for the new.

- What are the roles in your life you hold now? Parent, friend, teacher, professional, student, someone employed in a particular field, etc.
- As Jungian analyst Robert Johnson asks in lectures, *"Who are you coming on as?"* i.e., what are you telling people that you are?
- How do you think most people would describe you? Write down the first adjectives that come to mind—as many as you can. Are you happy with this description? What would you want to change, if anything?

Compare these words to what you put in the previous exercise where you wrote from the perspective of a friend. Any similar words?

FEEDING YOUR SOUL . . . OR DRAINING YOUR ENERGY?

A KEY part of "Capturing Today" is tapping into what the daily, fleeting hungers look like, and where current nourishment resides in your life. (This is a slightly different goal than Chapter 10: "Faint Calls and Small Voices." That chapter looks at more hidden and positive yearnings; these questions ask you to reflect on the quality of actual, current interactions.)

- Who or what is nourishing (helpful, expansive, life-giving) for you? What leaves you content, satisfied, peaceful?
- Who or what is "junk food," i.e. something that may feel good initially, but is essentially not in your best interest? What or who drains you as opposed to replenishing you?
- Does your environment nourish or hinder you?
- What was formerly nourishing, and is not any longer? Your answers could involve places, people, activities, etc.
- Where in your life is there a lot of nourishment, but for some reason you don't avail yourself of it? List people, activities, places, etc.
- Is there a "pattern of refusal" anywhere in your life? Things you know you need to do for yourself but don't feel deserving enough, or free enough?
- How are you bread for others, i.e., how do you nurture the people in your life?
- What are you yearning for? What needs and hungers do you have at this time?

- What moves and touches you? What's the setting?
- What are your "icons"—the things that assume significance, are evocative or "window-filled" for you? A retreat leader and monk once described icons as "Reminding symbols that remind us of what we tend to forget." What are your current icons? They could be objects, an aspect of nature, a piece of music or writing, etc.

GETTING GRAPHIC

As you answer these questions and transfer data to your Circle Pages, see if any of the answers come in the form of shapes, colors, pictures . . . things that might be icons for you. Look through magazines for pictures that "feed" you now. Try travel magazines and interior design magazines to see what outer and inner places are compelling.

LIVING *YOUR* QUESTIONS

AMIDST ALL the questions here that key off of various parts of your life, larger questions are also at work. These are the questions that are not so much descriptive as *pressing*: They pertain to what feels most important, most scary, most inescapable at a given moment. These are the questions that color our "todays" in ways we're often not aware of. They are the current mysteries we are wrestling with—or are wrestling with us.

In *Letters to a Young Poet*, Rainer Maria Rilke urged his friend to both love and *live* the mysterious questions in his life. He advocated embracing the questioning process itself, and was not caught up in speedy answers.

Examples of these type of questions are: Should I leave? Do I want a life of my own? Can I do this? Where should I move? Am I worthy? What do I love? Why am I here? How do I want to be remembered?

- Picking up on Rilke's words, what questions are you living? A little more insistently, what questions are living *you*? Another way of saying this is, what is *the* question in your life right now?

- What books, movies or music are you drawn to these days? Which are finding you, i.e. what is questioning *you*? What are you learning?
- From the author Simone Weil, a core question: "What are you going through?"

Remember that the very personal answers to these questions can be conveyed in words, symbols, pictures, any shorthand you prefer.

LISTENING TO YOUR BODY

THE KEY questions in our current lives don't just show up intellectually; our bodies are sources of information, as well.

- What signals has your body been giving you lately about your life as a whole? Stop and do a "body scan": Close your eyes and scan your body for tension, energy, heaviness, pain, joy. What shows up? Is your body questioning or affirming how you're currently living your life?
- Describe how you feel about your body. Are you exercising it? Is there a form of physical activity you want to add at this time?
- Do you have your ideal body? If not, what is keeping you from it?
- Is your body performing at optimum health? Has anything changed for the worse—or better—in the recent past?
- A wonderful poem by Mary Oliver called "The Wild Geese" has the line "You only have to let the soft animal of your body love what it loves." Where do you feel the "soft animal" of your body loving something? (This not necessarily about sexuality, but also about trusting instincts, or taking care of oneself in a physical way.) What is your body currently longing for? Rest . . . play . . . the woods . . . the sea . . . sleep . . . walking . . . meditation . . . a bath . . . a break?

WORKING WITH DREAMS

DREAMS BRING our physical bodies and our unconscious together, and enthusiastically take on the task of commenting on our "todays" in often inscrutable ways. The complex but rewarding task of working with your dreams is the subject of many other books, and we have listed suggestions for additional reading in the chapter "Resources for the Journey". We also cover dreams in Chapter 10: "Faint Calls and Small Voices."

Any "today" section of a Soul Map can glean good clues from your "tonight" meanderings. So if you are remembering your dreams lately, try to capture them:

- What recent dreams come to mind? What adjectives would describe them?
- What are the settings? What are your roles?
- What are the key images in these dreams? What are your associations with these images? Write down as many associations as you can think of. Which seems the most compelling at this time?
- Is a dream commenting on an aspect of your current life?

RETURNING:
Mapping What You Find, Dreaming the Future

DESCRIBING YOUR current life, your roles, what feeds you, what drains you, what you're wrestling with, feeling like, dreaming of—the traveling you have done in the "today" aspects of your life has been wide-ranging.

Now it's time to emerge from your answers to all these exercises and listen to them for the additional clues they may hold—for your "today" and also for your future. One of the first things to look for is what we call enlargement.

TRACKING THE WORK OF ENLARGEMENT

DEEP LISTENING processes like Soul Mapping often take us to bigger places—to a larger sense of what we can do and who we are. Amidst the stable elements that make up your "today" are intimations of change; scratchings at the door about ways you're being invited to grow; realizations of places that have become too small for you.

We're not suggesting you have to leap at every hint, or that change is always good or even necessary. But it is important to simply be aware of where, in your present life, you are being nudged outside your comfort zone. The nudges often show up as a creative tension between an old view of yourself and a new, more expansive or powerful one. Write down your answers to the following "tension locators" using both the data you have surfaced so far in this chapter and whatever thoughts come to you now.

- Where are you being pushed outside various boxes? Where are you currently being invited to stretch?
- Where are you currently being asked to come out of hiding? Where is enlargement at work in your life? Where are you being asked to learn something new? Are you resisting this?
- Is there an important task at this point in your life that you are avoiding? Why? What is the fear behind the avoidance?
- What's surprising you?
- What do you need to say "yes" to?
- Where do you need to say "no?"
- What are you tolerating?
- What needs to be cleaned up in your life?
- The poet David Whyte coined the term "courageous conversations" for those conversations that need to happen, but we are reluctant to have. What are the "courageous conversations" you need to have? With others? With yourself?
- Where are you stuck?
- What is most difficult for you to receive?
- In one of his books, Joseph Campbell asks, "What one thing would you want to add to your life? What would you want to take away?"

DON'T TAME THE TENSION

These "tension locator" questions are useful because they shine a high-beam light on places of discomfort, and discomfort often precedes growth. The temptation can be to see the answers as terrifyingly absolute, which can prompt responses like "It will never work." "I can never leave/change/do that." Resolving the tensions doesn't necessarily mean upheaval. It *does* mean listening to them and integrating them in some way, often in the face of massive procrastination. The chapters on fear, reading your map whole, and moving with your map will all help you move forward creatively with what you locate in this section.

WHERE ARE YOUR NECESSARY DEFEATS?

AS YOU reflect on all the ways enlargement is at work in your "Today," also look at the necessary shrinking or "taking away" that accompanies change. The Quakers have a lovely expression to describe change that happens naturally: "As way opens . . ." These are the moments when you push in a direction and things just flow; doors open.

But just as "way" can open, it can also close, and the Quakers know you can learn just as much from "as way closes." The doors you pound on that don't open, the paths that turn out to be blocked, the misassumptions made about people or situations—these shape our lives through *humility* in the best sense of the word: "Humus" means "earth," so the things that seemingly are defeats are also the clay that shapes us. The poet Rilke wrote that we grow not by winning but by being beaten "by greater and greater beings."

- What are your current defeats? What isn't working in your life? What hasn't happened that you had hoped for? Can you see any "defeats" where the loss unexpectedly opened the way to something greater or better?
- Are you called to give up anything now? To put something down, to stop struggling with something that has not worked out and make room for something else to happen? To let go?

SCANNING "TODAY" FOR FUTURE HOPES AND DREAMS

YOUR "TODAY" is a type of "home base." It's from the perspective of your feelings about your life today that you do exercises in the other Soul Mapping chapters. Your life today is also the bedrock where clues about future hopes and dreams first appear.

You did the exercises in this chapter from the perspective of the present. Now go back and look at your answers from the perspective of the *future* and see if there is anything you hope will change.

- Go back to the basic surroundings section and look at the adjectives you wrote characterizing your relationships with key people in your life. A month from now . . . a year from now . . . how would you like those relationships to be? What can you do today to help that come about?

Do the same projecting exercise for where you live, your communities, your work. If you see desire for change in any of these categories, what time frame would you want to make the change in?

- Look at your current roles. What roles would you love to have taken on in five years? In one year? What about next month? What can you do to get ready for these new roles?

- Linger over the answers to the questions about what fed or drained you. Three months from now, what do you need to have added to your life that is sustaining, and what do you need to turn away from?

- The question that is living you right now—if you were to really engage it, wrestle it to the ground, how would that shift your future?

- Also look at the tension locators—how would engaging them open up what you feel is possible in the near future?

- For a jump-start look at the future, try the "miracle" question from psychotherapy: "If you could wave a magic wand and make a wish, what would it be?" What would change? What would you be doing? Notice where your energy goes in your answer. Is there any way to work at this without the "miracle?"

DO YOU NEED TO MOVE YOUR FEET?

YOUR ANSWERS to the future visioning questions above—and to many of the "today" exercises—raise the question of what needs to change. It's interesting that the root for the word "hear" comes from the same root as the word for "obey." The whole question of how or whether to *act* on what comes up in a map is never far away in the Soul Mapping process.

Even though "Capturing Today" is the first component of your overall map, as some of your answers reveal, you don't have to do all the other chapters to have glimmers (or not-so-subtle whacks) about things you need to shift, rectify, jettison or add in your life. If that is happening as a result of doing this chapter, turn to the chapters in the book on moving through fear and roadblocks; viewing your map whole and going from "map to movement" for ways to work with what has come up. We encourage you not to skip the other chapters totally, since they add many pieces to the puzzle.

CONCLUSION

As a moving target, ever renewing, your "today" is never solved nor finished. While all of the Soul Mapping chapters and exercises bear repeat visits, the "today" chapter requires them. Reworking these exercises is a great way to stay in touch with the deep currents at work in you at a given moment.

A friend of ours, Marv Hiles, creator of a very soulful journal of daily readings called *The Daybook,* once wrote "Your fleeting life is where the eternal truth works." That "fleeting life" is what "Capturing Today" is after.

THE SOUL MAPPING METHOD:
TRANSITIONING TO THE CIRCLE PAGE

BY NOW you should have a lot of written or drawn feedback from your own creative self about how your life today looks and feels. Those pages, however many they are, are important; keep them in their entirety as you would any valuable journal, even as you condense them onto one of the ten Circle Pages that become part of your overall Soul Map.

As you transfer this information to your Circle Page, invite symbols, color, and pictures into the process even more. Look again at magazines and cut out pictures that touch on what you have written. See what color represents aspects of your "today." Look at which questions you welcomed, and which brought up resistance.

The Circle Page questions are designed to help you with this sifting and honing. Feel free to add others of your own. The key to the Circle Page is to pull out, in written or drawn from, the *essence* of the chapter for you. You may find yourself adding new insights as you do so. Just let them come. Most of all, let your circle take shape however it wants to. Emily Dickinson wrote: "My Business is Circumference." Let the Soul Mapping circles be places to lavishly, lovingly, and prayerfully inscribe your "business."

CIRCLE PAGE QUESTIONS

※

YOUR CIRCLE PAGE:
What "Angels Are Knocking?"

LOOK OVER all you have written for this chapter. Think of it as a particular journey unto itself, into very specific territory. You return from this exploration with many thoughts and impressions. As a way to start that honing and honoring process, answer these questions quickly and intuitively. You can write directly in your circle or answer the questions on another piece of paper and then transfer the results to the Circle Page. Either way, this is a place to record the most insistent (and possibly most important) data from your responses; a place to capture those "angels knocking at our doors," that D. H. Lawrence referred to.

- What masks or roles best describe you at this time in your life?
- What are you most excited about in your life right now?
- What are you most troubled by in your life right now?
- Where do you sense enlargement most at work in your life?
- What questions are most pressing right now? What questions are "living you?"

SACRED PLACE

OF ALL the answers to exercises in this chapter, which one(s) feel most sacred and important to you at this time in your life?

EMOTION

IS THERE a predominant emotion in your responses to the exercises?

SURPRISE

WHAT MOST surprised you about your responses in this chapter? What do you know now that you did not know before?

NURTURE AND RENEWAL

WHICH ANSWERS spoke the most to a hunger or a longing? Is there an aspect of your answers that, if it were more integrated in your life right now, would be particularly nurturing and helpful to you?

PERSONAL IMPERATIVE

A FAMOUS poem of Rilke's starts by gazing at the torso of Apollo, and in the last line pivots on the reader and says "You must change your life." As you review your answers to this chapter, do you sense any imperative arising from what you wrote—any need to change your life? If so, where is the urge for change most insistent in this chapter?

2

ECHOES OF AN EARLIER YOU
CHILDHOOD REMEMBRANCES
AND FAMILY PATTERNS

———— ೪ ————

"If you do not come to know the deeper mythic resonances that make

up your life, they will simply rise up and take you over . . . the myth will

live you."

—Joseph Campbell

GETTING THE LAY OF THE LAND

OUR CHILDHOOD is the soil of the soul, the ground out of which we grow and take shape. Those early experiences with parents and grandparents, siblings, cousins and classmates contribute much to our sense of who we are and our values and beliefs about the world. Since families play such important roles in our lives, shaping us in ways seen and unseen, it is crucial to track the ways the past is still at work.

So this chapter will cover a lot of vital territory, and include more than the usual number of exercises. You will look at your own childhood longings and clues, and also map the operating beliefs and values in your families. Exercises will help you think about ways your present family relationships often echo past dynamics or reveal hidden "patterns of loyalty" which can quietly and inexorably keep you on a course not entirely of your choosing. This kind of spadework is very important to the process of awareness and future possibility, and to the "openings" that Soul Mapping is all about. Our past continuously co-exists with our present, and in doing so, subtly influences our future choices.

A lot of these subtle childhood influences are hard to "get" cognitively; it's difficult to just sit and "think" about what they were. It can even be hard to surface childhood influences in therapeutic settings. The Soul Mapping exercises are designed to make elusive information surface; to tease out of you the images, remembrances and subtle dictates that still have a life of their own.

THE POWER OF CHILDHOOD INFLUENCES

WE ALL have stories of childhood influences—things that shaped us then, and continue to do so now. Making them conscious, honoring them, choosing to expand them, or to move beyond them is the work of this chapter.

These influences can lurk even amidst our best-foot-forward efforts at change. One client, Marion, came to work on career and personal issues and seemed very motivated. But shifts didn't happen, and there were always reasons, and "yes, buts" about why specific changes weren't ideal. One day, the counselor asked her to leap ahead—what was she supposed to be doing in, say, ten years? Immediately she answered with great clarity: "Oh, I'll have moved back to Ohio to take care of my mother." As the youngest daughter, she felt an unspoken—but inescapable—fate was out there; this role was hers in the family system, whether she wanted it or not. The role wasn't immediate, which gave her time to do something in the interim, but its unacknowledged acceptance subtly prevented her from going forward in everything she was trying to do in New York City.

These "patterns of loyalty" can be very subtle, and we can be the last people to see how they operate in our own lives. Yet they shape our trajectory and what we think is possible for ourselves.

There are many exercises and meditations that can bring to mind key aspects of your childhood. We have assembled a wide collection, and invite you to amplify on them, or to add our own. As always with Soul Mapping, the technique alone is not what's important; the goal is for you to tap into what's vital for you about this time in your life.

For some aspects of childhood, you will be bringing up things that may seem like "old baggage"—things you would rather let go of. By "letting go of old baggage," we don't mean passing judgment on your family or deeming all of your past unworthy. What we advocate is *awareness* of how unspoken and unconscious assumptions regarding life, work and what is possible or enjoyable get communicated from one family member to another. Some of these assumptions are useful; some aren't. The key is to be *conscious* of them, so you can make the decision to let them guide you—or not.

While it traffics in our "pasts," this is very much a chapter about the present and the future. As a journey unto itself, this chapter will chart past and present influences, all with an eye toward what readers desire for the future. How do you want to use the material here, born of the past, to shape the tenor of your future relationships with yourself, your family, your friends and companions?

BEGINNING EXPLORATIONS:
Surveying the Past and the Present

FAMILY WORD SKETCH

LIST THE closest members on your family tree, living or deceased: parents, siblings, spouses, grandparents, aunts, uncles, cousins—whoever was important in your life. Leave space around each name. Also include yourself.

Next to each name, write down the first adjectives that come to mind about that person. Don't be shy; this is private work. Was a parent happy, sad, intolerant, quiet, frustrating, frustrated, generous, distanced, angry, selfish, easygoing? Write down as much as you can for each person. Let the adjectives multiply, as they describe personality, orientation to the world, vocation, moods, etc.

EXPANDING INTO BELIEFS

LOOK OVER the adjective portrait you "drew" for each person. Can you amplify your description to include any beliefs or values that each person embodied . . . or proclaimed . . . or conveyed to you and to the world?

These beliefs and values are both subtle and common. Examples are:

- Ideas about what work is appropriate, acceptable, or expected.
- Proper roles for men and women in a marriage or family.
- Beliefs about the world: it's unfair; it rewards the just; it doesn't reward the just. Life is hard. Life is to be lived. Things get worse. No, they don't.
- Gender beliefs: Men tend to. . . . Women tend to . . .
- Religious beliefs, if any: God is a God who . . .

LOOKING AT RELATIONSHIPS

LIST SEVERAL adjectives about your parents' marriage(s), describing their relational style, level of intimacy, conflict approach, etc.

List some adjectives about your relationship with your parents and siblings, if any. Write whatever comes to mind, after doing the above exercises.

Let these words and phrases gestate for several hours, or even better, for a few days. Then come back and reflect on them and see what additional words emerge. Have you thought of other adjectives or characteristics you overlooked initially? It can take the subconscious a while to mull over questions like these.

THE FAMILY PORTRAIT

USING CRAYONS or colored pencils, draw a family portrait as it was when you were a child. Don't worry about artistic ability. Be spontaneous! Be noncritical as you draw. Come back to your portrait a few hours later and write down thoughts based on these questions:

- What are your impressions?
- What is your position in the portrait?
- Why did you draw it this way?
- What unconscious, unintended qualities exist in the portrait?

THE EMERGENT ADJECTIVES

Looking over all you have written so far, are there some words that keep repeating? Themes you keep underscoring? A few words that speak volumes? Jot them down here, as a way to capture them for the Circle Page later.

LUXURIANT REMEMBERING: RECAPTURING THE PHYSICAL

IT'S IMPORTANT to allow ourselves physical contact with childhood loves and desires. To the extent that this revisiting is possible, it is not just an exercise in nostalgia, but a source of strength, direction, fun and joy.

- What were your favorite activities, pastimes, landscapes?
- What music do you remember from your childhood? What feelings rush back when you hear it today?
- What do you remember about childhood daydreams? For some of us childhood was, in part, a time of fantasy and possibility and a luxuriant sense of lots of time on our hands.
- What pictures or posters were on your walls as a teenager?
- What were summer vacations like?
- How did you spend your free time as a child?

Is there anything here you need to literally reconnect with? A part of the outdoors, a favorite activity, or time spent daydreaming?

TRAVELING DEEPER:
Charting New Territory

THE INITIAL explorations in this chapter plunged you pretty quickly into a thicket of family associations and remembrances. We now want you to take what you gleaned from the beginning explorations and go even deeper, in some playful, wide-ranging directions.

TRACKING FEELINGS USING KEY WORDS

SOMETIMES ONE small word can trigger much remembering. Write a brief sentence for each of the following words, answering the question, "What was the place of ____ in your family?"

Nature	Illness
Anger	Tenacity
Joy	Feelings
Dancing	Animals
Reading	Learning
Food	Heroic Efforts
Sadness	Death
Passion	Desperation
Music	Compassion
Hugs	Secrecy
God	Wonder
Money	Fear
Art	Holidays
Solitude	Chaos/Order
Courage	Intimacy
Beauty	Laughter
Bodies	Grief
Privacy	Loneliness

Also: Were there any "forbidden topics" in your family—things it was understood were not to be discussed, or only discussed uncomfortably and rarely? List them. (They could include some of the above words.)

YOUR SIX FIXED IMAGES

OUT OF the tapestry of all the above exercises and the family sketch adjectives, we invite you to pull a few key threads: Close your eyes and ask yourself, "What are the six fixed images that have defined, shaped, or resonated in my life?" Imagine you have a huge photo album of your childhood and adolescence, and could only pick out six photos as representative. Which would they be? Why?

Feel free to capture these images with words, a color, or drawings. Look through magazines for a picture that might represent part of an image. Get out old photo albums and make copies of pictures that speak to you.

CHILDHOOD AND FAMILY: THE MYTHS START HERE

IN THE quote at the beginning of this chapter, Joseph Campbell urges us to make conscious the myths and trajectories that make up our family story. These are often subtle threads woven into the whole fabric of your life. Here are some ways to locate the important themes, whether unspoken or all-too-familiar.

THE STORIES OTHERS TELL:

- What stories do your parents or your friends like to tell about you from when you were younger?
- Which of these stories are you proud of, ashamed of, tired of?
- Were you compared to other relatives? In what way?
- Were your talents encouraged . . . or dismissed . . . or not noticed?
- Did your siblings get to do things you wanted to do?

THE UNSPOKEN HOPES AND DREAMS:

- Where are the mysteries in your own family? These can be unexplained developments, ways that things just "are," etc.

- Were there any journeys your parents were not allowed to take? These aren't necessarily literal journeys to a specific place; they can be about not being able to finish school, or work at a particular company, or pursue a beloved avocation, etc.
- Are there any journeys you have not been allowed to take; anything you have been forbidden to pursue, or discouraged from doing?
- Conversely, is there anything you are called to do, be, or finish? Is it a continuation of something a parent wanted for him or herself in some way?
- In your family, what were the dominant images of "the good life"? How do these images speak to you now? Do they motivate you?
- What roles were possible for you growing up?

ACKNOWLEDGING FAVORED ROLES AND GREAT EXPECTATIONS

WE ALL grow up under expectations, silent or voiced, about who we are to become or how we are to be. Author and Jungian analyst Marion Woodman points out that we may identify with our parent's roles for us initially, but then we have to figure out where *our* reality resides.

- What was your "role" in your family, i.e., little helper, troublemaker, silent one, good girl, responsible one, black sheep, commonsensical, daydreamer, Goody Two-Shoes, rebel, good student, etc.
- Ask your siblings or other relatives: What was your reputation in your family? How did they perceive you growing up?
- What did your family expect of you?
- What were their hopes for you as an adult?
- What was the unspoken agenda for you?
- Did either of your parents project their unfulfilled dreams onto you? What were those dreams?
- Did your family lack expectations for you? Why?

Anna went to public high school, worked hard and then got into a very prestigious Ivy League college. She excelled there; went to an top law school; clerked for a judge and worked for a large, respectable corporate firm. After some wrestling, she acknowledged her dissatisfaction with the law, left the firm, and she is now taking time to work in the non-profit sector and paint. She has had to confront the flattering but ultimately limiting role she now realizes she always played: "The best little girl in town." The one who excelled and worked the hardest, and achieved. (And who was afraid of not doing well.)

Just leaving the law won't allow her to leave this role behind; she will need to substitute, or at least add to, her repertoire of roles in order to approach her new work in a new way—in a way that is true to her self. In doing so, she will regain control of her life, freeing herself from the massive sets of expectations she's used to laboring under.

Taking back that control is more than moving in reaction to a past role. Going violently or abruptly in the opposite direction just proves we are still under the influence of that initial role. Midlife calls us to take an informed middle path, aware of the cost and promise of what shaped us, and able to choose for ourselves in ways that are creative, not reactive.

MY ROLE(S) AS I WAS GROWING UP WERE:

MY CURRENT ROLE(S) ARE:

Note your responses to these last two questions in a place you can find them again easily; we will be adding a third question regarding roles in the next section of this chapter.

THE WIDER CAST OF CHARACTERS

WHO WERE the "special" people in our childhood or adolescence who either helped or rescued you or served as alternative role models? Who gave you a sense of another world beyond your family system? What were their gifts to you? Did they "recognize" you in some way that was different from how your family saw you? They could be someone else's relative, a teacher, a neighbor, a peer's older sibling, a coach, an employer, a religious leader, a friend's parent, someone you read about, etc. Write down their names and why they were important to you.

MY KEY PEOPLE

WHY THEY MATTERED

PUTTING YOUR CHILDHOOD ESSENCE IN A PARAGRAPH

WRITE IN the third person a personal, descriptive paragraph about yourself as a child based upon the answers above. Use your childhood name. You might write from the perspective of your parents or other relatives, or from a teacher's point of view. Or write simply from a vague sense of how "adults" saw you then. Allow your imagination to rule. This can be a very surprising and revealing exercise. Write several statements if you wish.

EXAMPLE:

"Danny is a good boy who works hard and helps others and is frightened by teachers and peers. We expect him to become a teacher in a safe, secure environment, never to marry, and to live on potato chips and sour cream. We expect him to gain enormous weight but remain kind and jocular as he continually visits his poor dad."

This came from a client's imagination, uncensored. There are humorous touches, but they occurred naturally, as he just let himself write. In doing so, he got at some pointed and important hopes and expectations hidden amidst the details. He was not supposed to leave the Midwest (which he did) and he was not supposed to marry (which he also did). And he's not a teacher.

Which brings us to the whole issue of how childhood shapes vocation.

VOCATION CLUES BEGIN IN CHILDHOOD

MANY OF the exercises in this chapter are important tools as you ponder career and job possibilities, since the job search is not all in the present; what we consider, what opportunities we look at, how we imagine ourselves working . . . all can be profoundly and subtly affected by our pasts.

Carl Jung often pointed out that nothing affects a child so much as the "unlived lives" of his or her parents. If you are looking for a new or different job, you need to have a good grasp of your own family dynamics, and how they inform your assumptions and beliefs about work—and about yourself.

Many basic beliefs are formed and shaped in our families, not on the job, and if we're not careful these beliefs can become "facts." We can end up rejecting opportunities if we have no category to put them in, or wondering why we're following in someone's footsteps when we may not want to. For his first book, KEN had to get beyond the clear assumption that in his family system, "We don't do books." Selling retail goods . . . yes, but thinking and writing . . . no.

Here's another example of subtle dynamics at work: Rick grew up with a father who wasn't around, chiefly because he was working hard as a salesman. But Rick's father was never very successful, so money was scarce. Rick was determined to do it differently and steered himself toward a high-paying, demanding banking job that shaped him into someone who saw as little of his kids as his father had. This was the very thing he wanted to avoid; while he had escaped the money worries, there was what he called a "hellish repetition" from the workaholism, which Rick realized was based on the anxiety he also inherited from his father. Slowly, he started taking steps to take back his time without jeopardizing the job . . . and to create a new model for himself not unconsciously based on his dad.

Here are some "vocational" questions to think about and write answers to:

- What were your parents' attitudes toward their work?
- Did they love their work? Hate it? Were indifferent?
- What did they do? What about your other relatives—people related either by blood or by marriage?
- Did your parents change jobs frequently or hold onto the same jobs for years, or even their entire working lives?
- Did your relatives make mid-life transitions, change jobs, or divorce?

- What were your relatives' attitudes toward: men, women, marriage, schooling, money, work, success, finance, etc.? Jot down whatever you can remember about them and work. It can help to interview family members to get details.
- What were your family's values and beliefs about money, careers, ambition, job loyalty, risk-taking and "hard work?" How is "success" defined in your family?
- Were there gender expectations and limits? Are there types of jobs you would not have "permission" to do? Are there types of jobs that are expected or hoped for? What were you "supposed" to be and do?
- Are there any tragic aspects in your family beliefs regarding work? Did anyone fail at work or have to defer their dreams?

One of our clients did this exercise in one of our workshops, and was very startled to see that in her whole family tree, going back three generations, she was the only woman who had worked for pay. This seems like a very basic fact, but until she did this exercise, she had never realized how she was, from the family's perspective, trying to break new ground without any other role model. This "Aha" for her cast new light on her struggles to charge enough for her services, and other pertinent financial issues. It also gave that struggle a context. So she emerged not with an excuse, but with an awareness of an attitude that had subtly formed her that she needed to shake loose in order to go forward.

RETURNING:
Mapping What You Find, Dreaming the Future

CHILDHOOD MAY seem like it's all "said and done," but as any therapist will tell you, childhood dynamics are at work (and play) throughout our lives. Uncovering and working with them creatively is one purpose of this chapter; the other is to take what you have gleaned from the childhood exercises and use those insights to guide your future. Here are some additional exercises that take what you have done so far and ask you to *extend* the answers by thinking about future implications.

BREAKING NEW GROUND

YOU'VE NOW done a lot to uncover the family system you are from. One of our assumptions is that everyone, in the process of living the unique life he or she was born to lead, naturally has to make fresh tracks somewhere, to break new ground that may or may not be welcome news in your circle of family and friends. Think of the ways, large or small, you have done this . . . and ways you are called to do it now and in the future.

Mary is from a family system of long-standing marriages; no one has ever gotten divorced. This system of loyalty, intactness, and continuity with parents and grand-parents has been a gift . . . *and* a subtle, persistent deterrent, now that she faces the need to obtain a divorce from her husband. She has no one in her family to look to, consciously or subconsciously, to show her an alternative way to be. Just being *aware* of the power of the family norm has been enormously helpful to her.

- Does your family system reveal any new ground that you are trying to break? Is there anything you are trying to do that is different from how past relatives have handled things?
- Are you breaking any roles or patterns, either vocationally or in your personal life?

REVISITING CHILDHOOD CHAPTER "RESULTS"

THERE IS such a wide range of exercises in this chapter. While "Childhood" implies the past, we have touched on the many ways it still informs our present. Go back to some of your travels in this particular chapter and see how your answers can inform and shape your future days:

- "Family word sketch." Look back at the words you choose to describe members of your family. Think about the quality of the relationships you have with them now. Using adjectives again, what is the quality of relationships you would like to have with these people in the near future? What can you do now to bring that about?
- "Luxuriant remembering." When you recall the physical pleasures from your childhood that you journaled on earlier, are there any you can increase or add to your life now or in the near future?

- "Six fixed images." Remember your images from the past? Close your eyes and imagine the first six images from your future. Are they things you hope for? Fear? Are unsure of? Draw or write what you see.
- Acknowledging roles. Looking back at what you wrote about your roles growing up and current roles, add a third category—"Future roles I would love to step into are":
- What can you do now to help make those roles a reality?

HOLDING ON . . . LETTING GO

NANCY QUALLS-CORBETT, a Jungian analyst, commented in an interview that one of the tasks we face is "divestiture"—divesting ourselves of the false wrappings and roles we play out in our everyday lives.

After having done this chapter, what do you want to celebrate and hold onto or retrieve about your childhood . . . and what do you want to divest yourself of?

I WANT TO HOLD ONTO . . .

I WANT TO DIVEST MYSELF OF . . .

WHERE ARE THE STICKING POINTS?

SOME PARTS of childhood hang around long after we need them. Are people in your family, however lovingly, trying to keep you in an old way of being or an old stage you have grown out of? Are *you* the person keeping yourself in an old stage? Why? Try thinking of the tension in terms of cost and promise:

- The *cost* to me of staying in this old way of being is:

  Examples: I feel stuck, aren't growing, aren't happy, feel con-
  trolled, hemmed in, not true to self, etc.
- The *promise* to me of staying in this old way of being is:
  Examples: Don't have to risk anything, it's comfortable, it's famil-
  iar, I won't ruffle any feathers, won't fail, etc.
- Despite sticking points, in what ways have you taken a path different from family expectations and limitations?
- How have you surprised yourself?

CREATING YOUR CHILDHOOD SUMMARY PAGE

- YOU HAVE just completed a lot of work, dusting off childhood memories and circumstances you may have long since not thought about. Ideally, gathering all this information, perhaps for the first time, was a fruitful and perhaps surprising exercise.

You now have a wide range of data, emotions, recollections, etc. Keep it, add to it, use it in the future. And, for the purposes of creating your overall Soul Map, continue to hone in on what, after all you have remembered and written, is the most important for you: Turn to the Circle Page questions and reflect on what seems most vital from the chapter you have just completed.

As you transfer this information to your Circle Page, invite symbols, color, and pictures into the process even more. Look again at magazines and cut out pictures that touch on what you have written. See what color represents aspects of your childhood. Look at which questions you welcomed, which brought up resistance. Most of all, let your Circle Page develop however it wants to.

CIRCLE PAGE QUESTIONS

YOUR CIRCLE PAGE:
What "Angels Are Knocking?"

LOOK OVER all you have written for this chapter. Think of it as a particular journey unto itself, into very specific territory. You return from this exploration with many thoughts and impressions. As a way to start that honing and honoring process, answer these questions quickly and intuitively. You can write directly in your circle or answer the questions on another piece of paper and then transfer the results to the Circle Page. Either way, this is a place to record the most insistent (and possibly most important) data from your responses; a place to capture the "angels knocking" at your door.

- If you were verbally describing your childhood summary to someone, what would you tell them first?
- What feels the most inescapable?
- What is the most exciting?
- What do you identify with the most?

SACRED PLACE

OF ALL the answers to exercises in this chapter, which one(s) feel most sacred and important to you at this time in your life?

EMOTION

IS THERE a predominant emotion in your responses to the exercises?

SURPRISE

WHAT MOST surprised you about your responses in this chapter? What do you know now that you did not know before?

NURTURE AND RENEWAL

WHICH ANSWERS spoke the most to a hunger or a longing? Is there an aspect of your answers that, if it were more integrated in your life right now, would be particularly nurturing and helpful to you?

PERSONAL IMPERATIVE

AS YOU review your answers to this chapter, do you sense any imperative arising from what you wrote—any need to change your life? If so, where is the urge for change most insistent in this chapter?

3

LEARNING THAT ENLIVENED
Schooling and Education

—— ৵ ——

"I have come to see that knowledge contains its own morality, that it

begins not in a neutrality but in a place of passion within the human

soul. Depending on the nature of that passion our knowledge will fol-

low certain courses and head toward certain ends."

—Parker Palmer, *To Know as We are Known:
Education as Spiritual Journey*

Getting the Lay of the Land

THIS CHAPTER looks at the role of education in your life: what you have learned, what kind of experience it was, and how education is playing a part in your life now.

Why have a whole chapter on education in *Soul Mapping*? Formal schooling is an important aspect of your life to explore, in part because of all the time spent on it. Your "school years" can be a time of openness and naturalness in terms of realizing things about yourself and what you like to do; they can also be a time of grim memories about failure or competition that seem to limit your sense of what you are able to do now and in the future.

The Soul Mapping approach to education is part historical and part philosophical. This chapter will journey, as the others do, into the vital and linked terrain of past, present and future, this time using learning as the prism. It will encourage you to revisit your past experiences of education: what were the joys, difficulties and fears? In terms of the present, what are you learning now or longing to learn now? From those longings, what role can learning play in your future? Do you need to improve or acquire certain skills, explore a new area, step into a dream long deferred? Do you see the learning necessary for your future hopes as an opportunity or a deterrent?

In addition to exploring the role of education as a type of stepping stone, the Soul Mapping method embraces the true meaning of the word "education." The Latin *educare* means "to lead out of." It's not about experts stuffing you with information in a particular sequence. True education is about *leading* your knowledge, enthusiasms, and attributes *out* from you. Yes, mastery of new skills may be required, but the impetus for that work comes from the source that is *you*: your energy and interest in the topic.

If Soul Mapping is about listening to what new thing may be scratching at your door, about going in the direction of new life, then education can play a crucial role in the nurturing of any personal or professional change. Indeed, learning something new can be what ushers in the change you want to cultivate. It is also a great way to test new waters—to find out more before plunging.

If education is about leading what is most vital out of you, then it is a lifelong process. One of the joys of "adult" education, in fact one of the reasons why it is booming, is that people in mid-life have a very different experience of school than the average fifth grader. They choose to be there. Drawn by hunger for certain topics, they learn for the sheer fun of it, and often use education to make a vocational transition.

THE IMPORTANCE OF ALWAYS "BEGINNING"

YOUR ROLE as a "learner," past, present and future, is vital Soul Map data, since it can pinpoint new directions. Another reason we focus on education is more subtle, and it can show up in other chapters, too. Zen Buddhist practice has a wonderful expression: "beginner's mind." This desirable state has to do with not acting habitually, with perceiving what is happening with fresh eyes and reacting openly, ready to adapt and explore.

The "beginner's mind" orientation is often enhanced by learning: whether it's a new job or a new course or even a new relationship, it's not the same old terrain, and it makes us feel fresh, unsure, perhaps nervous. We are aware, in these times, that we are *learning*. There is vitality afoot, and opportunities for surprise.

Approach these exercises the same way: as a fresh time to play with and explore the role of learning in your life. They may well lead you to your next place of "beginner's mind."

BEGINNING EXPLORATIONS:
Surveying the Past and the Present

CHILDHOOD AS YOUR FIRST LEARNING GROUND

"BEGINNER'S MIND" very much describes a baby's natural learning abilities. During those earliest years a baby is a certified learning machine: There is nothing that is not of interest to a child if he or she is able to focus on it. One of the most fascinating times to watch babies is when they really do begin to focus on the world outside of themselves. Every object within reach holds their attention, every shape, every sound, and every movement.

This is the beginning of the lifelong learning process for the child. Besides being great fun, the child is learning how things work and how big people work. Her little mind is like a sponge soaking up every possible bit of information, a tabula rasa on which a whole life of learning will be written. The process starts out natural and easy and looks very different from the formal learning processes that take place at school, as well at the parental aspects of learning.

As the child gets bolder and bolder, she is bound to run into a few problems: glasses of milk spilled, crayons on the wall, and mud on the clothes all get varying degrees of disapproval from parents and other authorities. Time after time the real spontaneous opportunities for experimentation and learning begin to narrow, and we discover that there are right and wrong ways to do things. We also begin to hear labels like "dangerous" and "silly"—even "stupid."

DICK remembers this time in his life well: "My own parents were quite anxious about my education during my childhood. They were a fearful bunch anyway, but a newborn out-of-control kid presented all sorts of possibilities for disaster, and they kept me on a fairly short leash. Instilling fear was their favorite method of control; many warnings about actual and imagined dangers were presented in graphic detail. Some of it I heeded; much of it I ignored. I understand from family stories that I was one of the terriblest of twos, into everything. But as I look on it now, I think it was only one part willfulness, and three parts desire to learn. I wanted to know everything about my world and my body and what it could do."

SOUL MAPPING EXERCISE:

- ❧ Think back to your earliest attitudes about exploring your world. What do you remember? What stories did you hear in your family about how curious or exploratory you were? What kinds of trouble did you get into?
- ❧ What was your parents' attitudes toward learning in general? Toward you and learning? Was learning valued, worried about, not taken seriously, constrained, etc.?
- ❧ Are there any themes in these early learning experiences that exist today in your life?
- ❧ Did things happen back then to keep you from learning? How did you deal with it then? What about now?

THE SHIFT TO SCHOOL

SOMEWHERE AROUND our fifth or sixth year we hit what grownups begin to call the real learning experience: school. "Getting your education," "book learning," and other terms delineate the formal educational process from the one that had already been happening apace. We thought we were learning a lot, but when it was time to go to school, we were told the process was just beginning. Most of us were confused and not too thrilled by this change.

DICK remembers: "One difficult part for me was that all of a sudden there is this agreed upon body of knowledge that had to be learned and a number of difficult skills that had to be mastered. There were standards and tests, and there was also a certain amount of competition built in. Many occasions for feeling awful suddenly emerged, like the first time you were called upon and didn't know the answer, or the time you forgot to prepare something and found almost everyone else had done it. Most of us have quite a few memories of our grade school and secondary school experiences, and I know many of them are some of the worst feelings and sense of inadequacy we could ever imagine."

We can also have good memories: times we were excited about learning something new; a time we did well; a time we had fun with what we were learning. Most people have a blend of memories, good and bad. These memories do not necessarily remain in the past. They can shape our assumptions about what we are able to learn and do now and in the future. It's important to identify them, and see which are still at work.

QUICK . . . THINK "SCHOOL"

Before you start on the following questions, say the word "school" to yourself, and write down what immediately comes to mind. Let the words suggest other words. Your responses can have to do with school at any age.

SOUL MAPPING EXERCISE:

- ❧ What are your memories of grade school? Did you love it? Hate it? Were some years better than others? How did you feel about your classmates?
- ❧ Draw a picture of you at school at this age. What and who surround you? What is the mood in the picture?
- ❧ Think of both a good and a bad memory from your school years: grade school and then high school.
- ❧ What subjects were the easiest . . . which were the hardest? Any surprises here?
- ❧ What kind of *role* did you play in school? Did it change from grade to grade? For example, were you quiet and studious? A troublemaker? An athlete? What were your feelings about this role, whether it was how you saw yourself or how others saw you?

Emily, now in her mid-40s, remembers vividly the day in seventh grade when her particular school "role" took an unexpected turn. Up until then, she had done well in all subjects, including math. There was a sort of unofficial competition between her and Ann, a girl who also got consistently high grades. When called on in class, both Ann and Emily were known for giving the right answers. One day, the math which had been arithmetic veered into this thing called algebra, and Emily was instantly behind. Ann, as usual, was fine, and remained ahead of the curve. But Emily felt the lurch of falling backwards into a type of panic and a new role: classmates no longer looked to her as one of the really smart students.

Emily's new role was ultimately freeing and marked the beginning of her preferences for languages and English to show themselves. And it got her away from the spotlight of competition, which she hadn't liked. But she remembers the feeling of hitting the limits of her capacities in math as if it were yesterday, and that panic has precluded her from thinking she can achieve certain current goals, if they involve revisiting math.

❧ Did your roles shift as school went on?

❧ Were there subjects that defined you, either in terms of what you could do or what you thought you could not?

❧ Do these subjects have a current role in or impact on your life?

COLLEGE AND BEYOND

SHAPED BY the grade school and high school years, we move on to tackle the subject of learning as adults, whether in college, technical school, on the job, or later in graduate school. These first years as adult learners are important to the Soul Mapping process; they can indicate the first *choices* we made regarding subjects and areas that appealed to us, as well as our first need to defend those choices to family and friends.

SOUL MAPPING EXERCISE:

❧ If you did pursue learning in an academic environment after high school, what are your memories of your studies? Were you engaged, worried, bored, unsure, fascinated?

❧ What subjects drew you? Did you feel you "had" to take certain courses? Why? What courses did you like the least? The most?

❧ Do you feel you "wasted" or did not take enough advantage of the learning opportunities you were presented with years ago? What would you have done differently?

❧ Describe a favorite teacher or mentor. Gandhi has said that all education should be for the building of character. Were there some teachers who particularly shaped your character, maybe because they so loved what they taught that you caught some of their enthusiasm?

ॐ What about learning outside of school? What are your memories? How did you educate yourself in addition to what you learned in school?

ॐ What did you learn from any participation in sports, music, theater, the arts and other extra-curriculars?

In our private practices we often see people who were told by parents which educational experiences were okay to spend money on and which were not. This well-intentioned but disruptive advice often comes right at the time that nascent vocational plans are taking shape and wanting to take wing. The student with a knack for art history and a passion for design and teaching is pushed into law upon graduation because it's "professional." Result: He has utterly disliked what he has done for the past eleven years. The woman looking at graduate schools is told "Why do that? College is enough; just get a job and think about starting a family." (Yes, this still happens.) In other families, where relatives weren't able to finish their educations for various reasons, the impetus to go back to school in midlife can run up against the sense that education is a luxury you are not allowed to indulge in.

ॐ Did you have to defend your choice of major or vocational direction to your family? How did disapproval, if any, get handled? Did your family influence your choice of major? Does your family influence your current hopes and dreams about future education?

YOUR LEARNING SO FAR: A BIRD'S-EYE-VIEW

THESE INITIAL forays into the story of your education produce an overview of the role of learning thus far in your life. One of our premises is that, ideally, we are always entering new education territory throughout life. *Wherever you are right now, you are poised between what you have learned so far and how it has shaped you, and what you may choose to learn in the future.* The rest of the exercises in this chapter will go deep into explorations of what you're most drawn to now and where it might lead.

But first, here are some quick summary questions, born of the ones you have completed so far. Your answers will give you a sort of bridge into the next sections, a way to see how you currently view learning.

SOUL MAPPING EXERCISE:

ॐ What is your view of yourself as a "learner?" Positive? Negative?

ॐ Do you like to learn through books? Through actually doing something? Both?

- ▷ How has education defined you so far in your life? Freed you? Steered you? Told you what you most needed to hear?
- ▷ What books have been most pivotal in your life? How did they find you?
- ▷ How have you educated yourself in addition to what you learned in school?
- ▷ What is your best learning situation? (This can be any environment—academic, social, leisure-oriented, work-related, etc.)
- ▷ At this point in your life, what are your current settings for "learning?"

TRAVELING DEEPER:
Charting New Territory

THE MANY GUISES OF LIFELONG LEARNING

WE REMAIN learning organisms our whole lives, soaking up information we need throughout. But once out of traditional academic settings like college and graduate school, the impetus and the setting for ongoing learning become more varied.

In midlife, learning can be an engine for change, an indication of where we are stale, an imperative in transition. The ongoing appeal of education shows up in our enthusiasms and new hobbies, yes, but also in our work, in transitions both chosen and thrust upon us, and, especially, in what we have outgrown. The reasons for "lifelong learning" are many, and we have listed some below. Think of how these factors may be operating in your life now.

TRANSITIONS INCLUDE LEARNING

SHIFTS IN our life often require education around new topics. Graduation from school requires learning about the job market. A health crisis will prompt learning all you can about a particular illness. The Internet has revolutionized our ability to locate specific knowledge.

At its most basic level, this type of learning is about interested research: you are about to spend time in a country, so you read about it first. But often life deposits us in places we had no idea we were heading for, and amidst the shock comes a strong need to learn about this new land.

In her mid-30s, Nancy was busy at her advertising career of many years, not particularly satisfied, but with no real sense of what else was possible. "Learning" was something she had enjoyed—but that was for college, and those days were over. Her husband was extremely busy as an attorney, and their marriage seemed fine. Underneath, it wasn't so fine, and when she discovered he was having an affair, Nancy's current world dissolved and what was left was a chance to . . . learn. In an attempt to understand what had happened in her marriage, she became fascinated by psychology, religion and transitions. She became something of a midlife sponge for learning, taking classes and workshops she had not known existed. This was a new land. She realized her work no longer satisfied her, and she combined what she was interested in learning into a new vocation as a pastoral counselor.

Years later, she is quite clear that the learning, which was life-saving and thrilling to her, would not have happened without the initial loss. The irony is not lost on her. And the learning continues, as she adds to her professional skills.

SOUL MAPPING EXERCISE:

- ☙ Look back at the transitions in your life, chosen or not, happy or disruptive. Did these transitions precede any bouts of new learning for you? What do you remember about these liminal, unpredictable times?

- ☙ Looking forward a little, do you see work or lifestyle or developmental shifts coming—hoped for or inevitable—that would be helped by some education you could put in place now?

VOCATION IS THE CRUCIBLE FOR LEARNING

AFTER WE are out of school, for most of us work and family become the places where we are "educated." When you think about it, we start new jobs in that state of "beginner's mind"—not sure how things work, absorbing a lot of new information at once. Eventually, we become familiar with our work surroundings and expectations and we perform the job.

And then . . . and then . . . and then maybe nothing changes. Our bodies and minds, so used to courses that changed each semester, run up against the static quality of days without much new learning in them. We are not implying people need to be frantically ingesting new things every day. But there is a natural cycle in jobs that we see in the lives of our clients: A job is exciting and new at first, and demands on-the-spot learning. Over time, mastery eventually happens; people become "good" at what they do. This is satisfying—for a while. But then it becomes routine, and a certain stale quality can settle over the person and the job. Without being aware of what they are doing, people start to sabotage themselves at work: client calls don't get returned, reports get shoddy, etc. Many people who are "fired" admit quietly in counseling that they had a hand in the firing, through deliberate inattention.

This phenomenon at work has nothing to do with laziness and everything to do with staleness. The soul is longing for something new to learn. If you think of learning as a cycle, the starting point is newness and lack of knowledge about something. Then we move into more knowledge about the topic or the job, and then even more. It's paradoxical: at our point of most competence, we are most in danger of being bored.

This paradox does not mean we are doomed at our chosen work and must switch immediately, though it can be a precursor to a career change. It can also simply signal the need to shift the job in some way; to bring in new responsibilities; to get back some of the "beginner's mind" qualities.

SOUL MAPPING EXERCISE:

☙ Look at your current life, particularly your work. Where are you in the cycle of newness . . . adeptness . . . mastery . . . staleness?

☙ Have you outgrown any parts of your job? What can you do to bring learning into your current work situation?

☙ If you feel you have outgrown more than your job—i.e., you want to switch careers completely—what do you need to learn about in order to make that switch? The following section may be particularly helpful to you, if you are ready for a career change.

LETTING THE LEARNING FIND YOU

WHETHER YOU are thinking of switching careers, or just looking for the next thing you want to learn, listen to where the energy is. Do this playfully, ready to be surprised by the pull of something new . . . or the need to finally say "yes" to something long deferred.

SOUL MAPPING EXERCISE:

☙ Find a couple of adult continuing education catalogs from schools in your area. Peruse them as if they were a menu at a restaurant. See what's offered these days. Does anything attract or intrigue you? Does something surprise you, however impractical it might seem? Do any courses suggest new career directions? Or simply new directions your soul is hungry for right now?

This type of "catalog brainstorming" is vital, since often the new thing we need to do shows up externally first; it's easier to identify if we have an outside reference point, something like a catalog to react to.

George did the catalog exercise at a time in his life when he was tired of his work in legal research. All his schooling so far had been very cerebral, and he had certainly enjoyed it, but at thirty-five, he felt drawn to courses utterly unlike anything he had ever allowed himself to do: pottery, graphic design, watercolor. He literally needed to use his hands in this transition, to listen to them and not just involve his intellect.

Here's are some quick exercises to do before you get the catalogs:

☙ If you were dashing through an airport, and had nothing to read on your plane, but had time to grab three favorite special interest magazines from a huge newsstand, which would you pick? Do these interests represent things you want to learn more about? Does your work connect with any of these personal interests? Do you want it to?

☙ Imagine that at this point in your life you could go back to a school or learning environment designed just for you. What would be your "ideal curriculum?" List the blend of courses or topics or purposes.

NAMING THE THEMES

Look at your results from the above exercises. See if the courses "clump" in any way: Do they share themes, passions, or values? Course content can reveal where you want to "live" with your time, where your soul is hungry. What educational food do you most desire? Name the topics and themes.

RETURNING:
Mapping What You Find, Dreaming the Future

ASSESSING current or future transitions . . . thinking about learning on the job . . . brainstorming what new topics appeal to you . . . remembering the ones that always have tugged at you . . . you have worked deeply in this section to discover the learning that is most important to you.

Now is the time to emerge with your findings, highlight the most insistent themes on your map, and to think about how those themes and specific courses might enhance your future.

FOLLOWING THE DEEP LONGINGS

DICK ASKS the question: *"What would it look like to follow your own interests to their deepest conclusions?"* This is a profound way to extend the answers to the previous exercises.

SOUL MAPPING EXERCISE:

ℜ What would the "deepest conclusions" of your interests look like? Would it mean graduate school, writing a novel, switching careers, investigating an alternative religious tradition, visiting a foreign country?

ℜ What would your life look like in five years if you followed your interests to their deepest conclusions? What small steps can you take now to honor those "deepest conclusions?"

ℜ Since *educare* means "to lead out of," what part of you most needs to express itself now, and how can you use education to honor that part?

TESTING THE WATERS . . . BENCHMARKING SKILLS

TAKING A class is a great way to dip your toe in a new field or endeavor, as well as a way to acquire or improve skills in a new area.

SOUL MAPPING EXERCISE:

- ❧ What educational plans do you have?
- ❧ Have you set these plans in motion, or are you keeping them a secret, even from yourself?
- ❧ What courses do you want to explore at this time?
- ❧ How are they currently available—part-time, full-time, in person, via the Internet?
- ❧ Education as community: How would it be possible for you to plug into more communities that are built around the learning issues you are interested in?

DISTANCE BRINGS FREEDOM AND OPPORTUNITY

IN THIRTEENTH century China an entire caste of calligraphers had responsibility for the creation of all documents. These calligraphers made up their own profession. Their pictographs and symbols were so complicated that only a very few people could understand and use them. This was intentional—calculated to keep these elite professionals in control. In a sense our educational system in the past has been similar; scholars cornered as much as of the knowledge as possible, making the doctorate the rite of initiation, and keeping the highest and best information in the library stacks and the arcane journals of academe.

With the coming of books, and then the computer age, all that changed. The learning revolution continues with the Internet and distance learning, making it more possible and more compelling than ever to follow our longings for learning.

CREATING YOUR EDUCATION CIRCLE PAGE

YOU NOW have a wide range of data, emotions, recollections, thoughts and hopes around education. Keep it; add to it; use it in the future. And, for the purposes of creating your overall Soul Map, continue to hone in on what, after all you have remembered and written, is the most important for you: Turn to the Circle Page and jot down what seems most vital.

C. S. Lewis once wrote that the things we love to do and learn about may well be "bound together by a single thread"—a common quality that even friends and family may not see and that may be hard for us to put into words. It is there nonetheless, this thing we are "born desiring," that we watch and listen for. He describes it as "the secret signature of each soul."

As you reflect on all your answers in this chapter and move into the Circle Page questions, listen for that single thread . . . now, and in all your learning experiences to come.

CIRCLE PAGE QUESTIONS

❧

YOUR CIRCLE PAGE:
What "Angels Are Knocking?"

LOOK OVER all you have written for this chapter. Think of it as a particular journey unto itself, into very specific territory. You return from this exploration with many thoughts and impressions. As a way to start that honing and honoring process, answer these questions quickly and intuitively. You can write directly in your circle or answer the questions on another piece of paper and then transfer the results to the Circle Page. Either way, this is a place to record the most insistent (and possibly most important) data from your responses; a place to capture the "angels knocking" at your door.

- What were the early elements of your learning experiences? Positive, negative?
- Which experiences in school in the early years were the most determinative?
- What was your absolute best learning experience?
- What blocks do you have regarding learning?
- What are your future hopes and dreams with regard to learning and knowledge?

SACRED PLACE

OF ALL the answers to exercises in this chapter, which one(s) feel most sacred and important to you at this time in your life?

EMOTION

IS THERE a predominant emotion in your responses to the exercises?

SURPRISE

WHAT MOST surprised you about your responses in this chapter? What do you know now that you did not know before?

NURTURE AND RENEWAL

WHICH ANSWERS spoke the most to a hunger or a longing? Is there an aspect of your answers that, if it were more integrated in your life right now, would be particularly nurturing and helpful to you?

PERSONAL IMPERATIVE

AS YOU review your answers to this chapter, do you sense any imperative arising from what you wrote—any need to change your life? If so, where is the urge for change most insistent in this chapter?

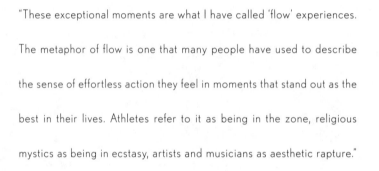

4

WHEN TIME FLIES
PLEASURES, PASTIMES AND HOBBIES

❧

"These exceptional moments are what I have called 'flow' experiences.

The metaphor of flow is one that many people have used to describe

the sense of effortless action they feel in moments that stand out as the

best in their lives. Athletes refer to it as being in the zone, religious

mystics as being in ecstasy, artists and musicians as aesthetic rapture."

—Mihaly Csikszentmihaly, *Flow*

GETTING THE LAY OF THE LAND

JUST AS what we are drawn to learn can lead us into professional and personal change, the things we love to do—our pastimes, hobbies, and avocations—can point the way to new possibilities. Even if you do not invoke change per se, tracking this chapter's pleasures helps you pinpoint the things most restorative to your soul now, as well as ways to expand your talents in the future.

The purpose here is to track the joys—the sheer pleasures, the things we do most naturally, and the things we can't help but do. It's important to literally give these pleasurable parts of our lives a place on the map, since they are often the first things that get cut in our schedule when we're under pressure or in a transition. From a balance perspective, this chapter can remind you of key sources of energy and embodiment.

Your answers here can hold clues to future directions. From a vocational perspective, these exercises can help you to see where your natural talents lie, for we often discount the things that come "easily" and think work has to be something we "work" at.

This chapter is not only about enjoyment, but also about *engagement*—those moments when all of you is engaged in an activity. The whole purpose of Soul Mapping is to engage you in various aspects of your life and to see that life whole. Listening for where you are most deeply *in* your life, what you most enjoy, is a vital part of the process.

REMEMBERING TIMES OF "FLOW"

SOUL MAPPING asks you to go back, through intuitive exercises, and engage various aspects of your life in a way that is thoughtful, playful, and unpredictable. It guides you into a re-connection with what moved you then, how it moves you now, and how it might move you in days to come.

There is a quality of "flow" to the entire Soul Mapping process, in that it seeks what is deeply true about you. Doing the exercises may not be the "effortless action" Mihaly Csikszentmihaly refers to in his book *Flow*, but they are designed to get at what is most vital in your life, to capture what stands out.

While all of Soul Mapping is designed to help you connect with that kind of depth, this chapter gets very concrete about the activities that feel particularly true to you. They may involve something you do at work. They may be strictly after-hours or weekend loves. They may be childhood pleasures you have long put on a back burner. They may be things you plan to defer until you retire. What these activities have in common is what DICK calls "The vertical quality . . . the depth. Flow activities provide pleasure in the deepest sense. On the surface they may look like nothing at all. An artist is carving a block of wood, a plumber is laying pipe, or a baker is baking loaf after loaf of bread. But each person is lost in thought, absorbed, engaged in movement that is a type of meditation."

RE-CREATION BEGINS HERE

THERE IS another aspect of this chapter's topic that goes way beyond anything conveyed by the word "hobbies." Doing something we are deeply connected to is recreation all right, in the sense that we are literally "re-creating" something that is life-giving, however casually or playfully. The dictionary reminds us that "recreate" is the work of reviving, refreshing, giving new vigor to something, especially after a time of work or exhaustion.

The gift of recreation is a form of healing. It relaxes us, and gets us off our usual conscious focus. Delving into particular hobbies, learning a new skill, winning a game, we get a sense of accomplishment. Immersed in these favorite activities, we are connected to life in a vigorous way, which reduces anxiety and gives us a certain exhilaration and a sense of gladness at being alive.

Flow experiences—whether they occur in our work or in pastimes—are more important than we usually give them credit for. In many ways they make our life worth living, bringing us into the present moment. They also help us keep our perspective as to what is important. Most of us will not come near the end of our lives wishing we had spent more time at the office. But most of us might wish we had spent more time in recreation.

----------☙----------

BEGINNING EXPLORATIONS:
Surveying the Past and the Present

CHILDHOOD AND TEENAGE BLISS

START YOUR explorations of what you deeply enjoy by remembering what captured you as a child and teenager.

SOUL MAPPING EXERCISE:

☙ What did you really enjoy doing with your leisure as a child? As a teenager? Are these activities still an important part of your life?

☙ How have your favorite activities shifted over your life?

When I was 5, I loved to:

When I was 10, I loved to:

When I was 15, I loved to:

When I was 20, I loved to:

When I was 30, I loved to:

When I was 40, I loved to:

ᑂ What themes or key words jump out at you from the list above?

ᑂ Look at the list above. Are there any activities that were once important to you that you
realize you would like to add back into your life in some way?

CURRENT INDULGENCES: ARE YOU SOMEONE WITH HOBBIES?

WHAT IS this thing called a hobby? DICK describes it at "something that is done
usually for fun, for pure pleasure. It usually has a particular knowledge base, maybe
a journal or two, and even a few clubs of like-minded people who enjoy the same
thing. The thing about hobbies is you know one when you see it."

SOUL MAPPING EXERCISE:

ᑂ What are your current pastimes or hobbies?

ᑂ What new hobbies are vying for your attention now?

ᑂ What would your favorite pastime be if you had the time for it . . . if you gave yourself
permission to engage in it?

> ### ATTITUDE CHECK
> Pause here for a quick check on how you feel about this chapter's topic, and our
> emphasis on the importance of re-creation. Clients have found these exercises
> revealing, for they can pinpoint two things: 1) The activities that you most enjoy;
> and 2) A deep-seated sense that you don't deserve to do them . . . or don't have
> the time . . . or they aren't really that important, etc. This chapter can even seem
> frivolous or indulgent to those who are really squeezed in their personal and pro-
> fessional lives. (Which of course is all the more reason to heed the chapter's call.)
>
> *continued*

So do a quick check: Jot down your attitudes around free time . . . play . . . hobbies . . . fun. See what words come up. These words and attitudes will govern how you view and respond to this part of your Soul Map—and this part of your life. Do you need to change any of these attitudes? Is this a part of your life where you are starving . . . or over-extended . . . or timid . . . or supportive?

As you ponder what words just came up, we invite you deeper into the subject matter.

✧

TRAVELING DEEPER:
Charting New Territory

WHEN DOES TIME FLY?

IN ADDITION to pinpointing specific activities that you love, this chapter is also looking for those times in your life when the entire *process* of what you are doing takes on a deep, focused quality. This kind of embedded concentration is ideally a state you access when doing some of the Soul Mapping exercises. It's not about doing something perfectly; indeed, part of the joy of fun and leisure is the chance to make mistakes, to take your time at something.

DICK describes the "flow" he achieves when engrossed in one of his favorite activities: clearing brush on some land where he lives. "The process is very simple. I go out in the morning and sit awhile thinking or intuiting what to tackle next. Then I set about methodically, stacking twigs to be burned during the winter months, cutting poison ivy vines and other parasites I have decided to ban from my garden. Hours pass by as I cut and stack, lift and pile, trim and carry. Anyone watching would think some kind of religious ritual was in progress, and I guess they would be right. There does seem to be a certain sacrality to the task.

"And while I am doing it the time just goes, and my mind and heart are at work too. Inner work is being done as well as the outer work. This is the real importance of it for me. The ritualized outer sameness somehow provides a channel through which all kinds of ideas and thoughts proceed when the mind is not cluttered. I often feel as if I am working on the grounds of a monastery, and the work is just a vehicle for the movement of some sort of spirit of God. Some of my best ideas and most heart-felt conclusions come during these moments."

SOUL MAPPING EXERCISE:

- 8• When does time fly for you?
- 8• Are there times when do you feel "uncluttered" and like a channel for ideas and thoughts? What are these times?
- 8• What are your favorite moments of "re-creation" outside of work? The times of "flow"—when you feel like you're really in the process of life, and being who you are supposed to be? Describe that person. What are your feelings? Can you draw or find a picture of how you feel when you are in that experience?
- 8• What do you do that is structured enough that it allows you to be "mindless" and relaxed while you do it?

THE HOBBY OF SILENCE

As DICK's brush clearing example showed, deep leisure experiences aren't necessarily about finishing something—there will always be more things for him to clear. Like meditation, his outdoor work is more about losing himself in order to find himself.

"Time flies" in ways that heal us when no so-called productive activity is involved; indeed, very important leisure activities, especially in times of transition, include walking, meditating, just being silent and staring out a window.

SOUL MAPPING EXERCISE:

- 8• Where is your recreation hunger now—particularly recreation that would be healing and relaxing for you? Taking the word "recreation" seriously in terms of its connotations of refreshment and renewal, what renewal do you most need now? We spoke in the last chapter about the times when transition **makes** us learn something, take on a new part of life. Recreation is about **choosing** rest, renewal, newness, enjoyment. How do you need to do this now?

> ### LET THE PHOTOS FIND YOU
> Read over your responses to all the exercises so far. Go to a large newsstand and look for magazines that appeal—they may be hobby- or travel-related, or general interest magazines. Buy a few and look for the photos, in ads or articles, that capture what you love to do . . . what you would love to try . . . what you long for in terms of recreation. Cut them out and save them for placement on your Soul Map. You may even be surprised by what new images speak to you.

"RESPONSIBLE FOR TIME"

"HOBBIES" ARE really about our relationship to time and to enjoyment. People think the issue around leisure time is that there isn't enough of it, and that is often true. But lurking on the other side of not enough time is the specter of time we are actually free to fill, and it can be a scary thought for many.

One of DICK's clients faced a transition that illustrates this discomfort with leisure. He relates:

"Jane is a woman who has had a very successful life. She has worked for many years as a lawyer in a large New York law firm. Very proud of the fact that she made partner in the days when women were hardly ever lawyers, she has worked long hours. She gave up the idea of marriage and a family, not so much as an intentional choice, but in the push and pull of her profession, she often had to make decisions that made relationships and the idea of children remote to impossible.

"Jane came to me one day on the verge of mandatory retirement, quite upset at what lay before her. She had saved plenty of money over many years of high salaries and no time to spend it. She also had a fairly good circle of friends, cultivated over many years of being single and needing some companionship on the weekends. But now, she wailed, what am I going to do with my time?

"Like many people, she had given others the responsibility of deciding how she spent her time. She deferred many pleasures, and even had to beg off many social opportunities because of her job, which had the highest priority. She literally did not know how to manage her own time and life. All of a sudden she had more time than she knew what to do with, and worse yet, had the total responsibility for structuring it, or living with time in an unstructured state.

It is this lack of structure that bothers a lot of people. Hobbies can help many of us fill our time with things we truly enjoy. Many people have a negative idea about hobbies. They see them as silly and lacking in the serious purpose that their jobs have had. Hobbies also do not have that imposed structure that a job has, and many people have never learned to respond to inner cues and desires, but have always done what is needed and expected.

What a difference, when people start to structure and take responsibility for their time! When Jane turned the switch in her brain from external to internal, she found she had all kinds of ideas about what she wanted to do. As she found out that these inner-directed ideas were just as engaging and important, or more so, than what she used to do, she became a very lively convert to a life of self-directed goals and activities. If anything, she is much more connected to her life than ever before."

LEISURE IS ABOUT KNOWING WHAT YOU WANT

AS JANE'S story illustrates, "leisure" can be an essential, rigorous developmental task that requires you to listen very deeply to an internal source of desire. Unlike most schooling and work, it is self-directed, and the responsibility starts and stops with you.

SOUL MAPPING EXERCISE:

- ෴ If you suddenly had a free month to fill, what would you do? Is there any way to incorporate some of your answer in your life now?
- ෴ Quickly jot down what you have done or do that is self-directed and stemming from inner desires, and what has its source in outer demands and directives. A key here is a blend, a balance. Of course there are things we have to do; the question is, are they joined by the things we love to do?

—— ᘔ ——

RETURNING:
Mapping What You Find, Dreaming the Future

KEEPING AN EYE ON YOUR "TRUE NORTH"

THIS CHAPTER is not just an exercise in vacation time dreaming . . . of listing all the things you wish you could do but don't have time for. In these exercises you have listed the very things that most bring you health and vitality; they are worth keeping an eye on, as a sort of "true north" that helps you find your way home when tired or lost. There is probably a physical component to what you have listed. What does your body enjoy doing?—whether it's a form of exercise, a type of outdoors activity, or just the time to be in nature and contemplate a particular landscape. You may have also hinted at future directions, either in your personal or professional life.

How you use your pastimes to help your future goals is this section's purpose.

LISTENING FOR TRANSITIONS

AS YOU do other Soul Mapping chapters, particularly the "Capturing Today" chapter, listen for transitions that are at your doorstep now, or that are whispers in the offing—bidden or not bidden, hints of change to come. Work may be shifting; a relationship may be beginning or ending; a parent or child may need special tending. Transition times are when we most need the restorative qualities of what we love to do.

LINKING LEISURE TO WORK

EVERYTHING YOU wrote here may be strictly about hobbies, or weekend time, or just doing things for the sheer fun of it. Which is fine. But before finishing this chapter, look over your answers and see if there are any hobbies or pastimes that might be the seed for a new vocation or avocation. Many times our hobbies are so ripe for changing into something more significant that we often miss them standing there right in front of us. Perhaps our hobbies are sending us strong signals of the next best thing for our lives and we didn't even notice! Look for clues even in what you consider your most insignificant hobbies. It is possible that gold is buried there.

SOUL MAPPING EXERCISE:

ᛅ Are there any vocational longings in your hobbies? If so, take what you love to do . . . or do well . . . or long to do . . . and ask yourself: Are people paid to do any aspect of this in the world? What do they call it professionally? Am I interested in finding out more about how people get paid to do this thing I love?

SUMMARIZING YOUR HOBBY HISTORY

THE EXERCISES you have done in this chapter constitute a compelling "timeline" of what feeds your soul the most. Now take some time to look at these activities as a group.

SOUL MAPPING EXERCISE:

ᛅ Look over all the favorite activities you have listed in this chapter. Do you see a thread? A direction? Some common elements? List them.

ᛅ Is something missing? Any thwarted hobbies? Or a "dream hobby" you have always wanted to begin? What do you want to add . . . explore . . . test?

Just as important, what do you want to drop—because you have too much going on, and not enough room for the conditions that assist flow—silence, slowness, etc.

ᛅ How do these hobbies fit into the puzzle of your life? Of the ones which you want to begin, which ones could be done immediately and which ones will take more time to begin? Which hobbies are pursued alone, and which involve other people?

ᛅ Pretend you were forced to retire this week; which of your hobbies would you most want to call into action?

SURROUND YOURSELF WITH SIGNS

THROUGH THE hobbies we long to do, the unconscious authentic self often speaks. Even if you are not able to begin a new activity now, or engage a favorite one as much as you would like to, it's important to surround yourself with reminders of these times of "flow" and deep connection. Symbols of your favorite activities can feed you when you are not actually doing those activities.

Look for a photograph, an object, a piece of music, a poem . . . some symbol that reminds you of your pastime. Put it in a prominent place where you live. Add to your collection as you add to your pleasures and pastimes.

CREATING YOUR PLEASURES AND PASTIMES CIRCLE PAGE

YOU NOW have a wide range of data, emotions, recollections, thoughts and hopes around hobbies and pastimes. Keep it, add to it, use it in the future. And, for the purposes of creating your overall Soul Map, continue to hone in on what, after all you have remembered and written, is the most important for you: Turn to the Circle Page and jot down what seems most vital. Cut out photos that make these activities even more vivid and accessible and use them on your map.

CIRCLE PAGE QUESTIONS

~ॐ~

YOUR CIRCLE PAGE:
What "Angels Are Knocking?"

LOOK OVER all you have written for this chapter. Think of it as a particular journey unto itself, into very specific territory. You return from this exploration with many thoughts and impressions. As a way to start that honing and honoring process, answer these questions quickly and intuitively. You can write directly in your circle or answer the questions on another piece of paper and then transfer the results to the Circle Page. Either way, this is a place to record the most insistent (and possibly most important) data from your responses; a place to capture the "angels knocking" at your door.

- What themes have emerged for you in this chapter?
- How do hobbies and pastimes fit into your life?
- Do your childhood hobbies come into the present or have you sprouted new ones?
- How do these hobbies and pastimes fit into the meaning of your life?
- What resistances do you have to passing time in pleasurable ways?
- What new hobbies are calling you at this time in your life?

SACRED PLACE

OF ALL the answers to exercises in this chapter, which one(s) feel most sacred and important to you at this time in your life?

EMOTION

IS THERE a predominant emotion in your responses to the exercises?

SURPRISE

WHAT MOST surprised you about your responses in this chapter? What do you know now that you did not know before?

NURTURE AND RENEWAL

WHICH ANSWERS spoke the most to a hunger or a longing? Is there an aspect of your answers that, if it were more integrated in your life right now, would be particularly nurturing and helpful to you?

PERSONAL IMPERATIVE

AS YOU review your answers to this chapter, do you sense any imperative arising from what you wrote—any need to change your life? If so, where is the urge for change most insistent in this chapter?

5

CULTURE THAT CAPTURES
TRACKING THE STORIES
YOU'VE LIVED—OR WANT TO

———— ❧ ————

"To live our own myth, to encounter all the aspects of ourselves, to

meet the realities of life's situations . . . is to keep related to the eter-

nal source in and beyond us. This is the living water."

—Elizabeth Boyden Howes, **The Choice is Always Ours**

GETTING THE LAY OF THE LAND

THE SOUL Mapping technique tracks various "essences" of us, and tracks them over time, noting shifts and possible new directions. One seemingly indirect way to pinpoint shifting energy is very revealing: to look at the culture—the books, songs, movies, television shows, plays, etc.—that spoke to our souls at different periods in our lives. It's fascinating and revealing to float up and analyze the characters, however fictional, who appeal to us; the heroes and heroines we admire; the plots we got lost in; the stories we yearn for.

What begins as an exercise in nostalgia is really a classic and fun type of "inkblot" test: the stories that were pivotal and essential at certain points in our lives reflect important facets of who we were then: how we saw the world; what our fantasies, hopes and assumptions were. In essence, they were our personal myths, and this chapter is about tracking those always evolving myths.

WHERE THE FUTURE FIRST SHOWS UP

THINGS IN the culture we're attracted to often presage shifts before we're even aware of them. We may be attracted to a new "story" but interpret it with the images and vocabulary of what we identified with at an earlier stage. The new story drawing you—or the silly, "impossible" one—may indeed be a type of call, and this chapter will help you hear those calls of the soul.

Though all the chapters in *Soul Mapping* encourage playful, open and spontaneous responses, this chapter really depends on them. At first, it can seem awkward (or weirdly and wonderfully natural) to come up with the characters and stories that aren't you and yet . . . in some way *are* aspects of your personality. So we've included a variety of exercises to help you brainstorm them, especially the stories that may be living you, as well as some background on why this part of Soul Mapping is so pivotal.

" C U L T U R E " S P E A K S
T O O T H E R C H A P T E R S

A note on doing the exercises: Please realize that many of the exercises in this chapter apply to other chapters in the book—particularly the chapters on childhood, envy, and faint calls. "Results" of these exercises can rise up from these other chapters, or can be applied to those chapters. So let the chapters bounce off each other and inform each other. And of all the chapters, it's especially important here to try to relinquish control over what comes up. Let yourself daydream, play, invite, and let go, without censure and with celebration.

WHAT STICKS TO YOU? CULTURE AS AN ENERGY LOCATOR

OF ALL the cultural offerings available to you over a lifetime, some appeal and some don't. Some movies capture your imagination; some leave you cold. Some types of books or magazines draw you; some annoy. Your response as a consumer of culture is unique; it is in itself a "map," a reflection of conscious and uncon-scious preferences.

Some cultural experiences are fleeting, but others become touchstones for human attributes, a type of shorthand unto themselves. Shakespeare's Othello is a familiar, tragic model for the jealous spouse; Hamlet and indecisiveness go together; Willy Loman in *Death of a Salesman* haunts us with the picture of a thwarted life. Hollywood romances by the dozen promise the happiness that sup-posedly follows finding the right person.

We often emphasize in this book the importance of listening for the symbols that also express key data from a chapter in your life. Sometimes those "symbols" are sto-ries, figures, concepts, myths, or fantasies from popular culture. The word "fantasy" comes from the Greek word for "a making-visible." Tracking the stories we've lived, or want to live, is a way of making visible some deep clues embedded in fantasies.

In his work on myth, Joseph Campbell stressed this way of "reading" ourselves when he said that mythology helps us identify the "mysteries of the energies pour-ing through you. Therein lies your identity." This chapter is about looking for the stories that currently carry energy for you—not just as a way to understand the past, but to grasp the tenor of the present and glean ways the future is calling. Calling these stories—these treasures—forth from a deep place will mean engag-ing your unconscious.

A NECESSARY DETOUR INTO THE UNCONSCIOUS

SOUL MAPPING takes seriously the existence of an unconscious, without further refining that concept along any particular psychoanalytic model. Many of the exercises in this book depend on engaging the reader's unconscious, either direct-ly or indirectly. Jungian analyst and author Robert Johnson has described the unconscious as a collection of unseen energies and distinct personalities; the secret source of much of what we think and feel.

This chapter is not about mastering the unconscious, or reducing it to a movie plot. But it *does* hope to tease out some of the powerful and perhaps unfamiliar aspects of your unconscious, by freeing you to identify with certain stories. In doing so, this chapter celebrates the basic Soul Mapping premise that we are always "bigger" than we think we are; that there many parts of ourselves that need to be honored, heard, or acted on.

BEGINNING EXPLORATIONS:
Surveying the Past and the Present

STARTING THE SEARCH: WHAT STORY IS LIVING YOU?

YOU'RE EMBARKING on a hunt for *patterns*: The word "archetype" refers to the powerful cultural patterns that are in the world and that also shape us. "Mother" is an archetype with vast associations, but many others exist, subtle and prevalent: the good girl, the successful businessperson, the playboy, the excellent student, the romantic dreamer, the dependable child, etc.

Before we start with exercises that link patterns to you through culture *you* liked, take a moment to ask yourself what is it that *others* affirm or project about you.

SOUL MAPPING EXERCISE:

- ❧ How would your friends describe you? What broad brush stroke descriptions would be at the top of their lists? Often, without being aware of it, we live into the attributes or hopes voiced by other people.
- ❧ Robert Johnson has written: "All of us have many distinct personalities coexisting within us at the unconscious level . . . Some are written all over us . . . Some are potentialities." What personalities are "written all over you"? What are the "potentialities" that you intuit that maybe people don't see but you know are there?
- ❧ What story is living you? How to find out? What movie or book or play has grabbed you lately? What, in the words of one friend and writer, "clings like Velcro"?

COMPARE YOUR FAVORITE STORIES FROM THE PAST . . .

ONE WAY to see how you are changing is to compare what from our culture appealed to you some years ago with what appeals now. This is basic, revealing soul movement that can otherwise remain hidden or hard to articulate. Inner shifts can be more visible if pegged to an outer artifact. For example:

When asked about favorite books or movies from her past, Helen, age forty-two, immediately thought of the two movies she had seen multiple times: *Casablanca* and *Sleepless in Seattle*. She described them as perfect for the "hopeless romantic" and "sentimental slob" she felt she was. These movies provided delicious emotional experiences for her, reinforcing a view of relationships she described as "shimmery," and "magical." These were her cultural picks from her late twenties and early thirties.

SOUL MAPPING EXERCISE:

What book, TV show, story, drama, myth, etc. appealed to you in the past? What resonated for you some years ago? Close your eyes and relax, and see what comes up first. Jot it down, along with why the story was so compelling. Do more than one if you can.

In the workshop where she did this exercise, Helen reflected that these movies were very much about the search for a soul mate and how paramount that seemed; the quirks of fate and romance; the intense focus on what happens to people in love.

. . . WITH YOUR EMERGENT STORIES

SOUL MAPPING EXERCISE:

Now shift to the present: What book, TV show, story, drama, myth, etc. appeals to you *now*? Often these stories will be very different than past ones, because they track what is emerging in you. Again, jot down whatever first comes to mind, and why.

When Helen did this part, she immediately thought of an autobiography she was reading by a psychoanalyst. The author is a wise, introverted, creative man doing fascinating work with focus and grace. He never married, and clearly honored the interior life, solitude, his dreams and his work with clients.

Helen described the shift from the movies in her twenties to this book as the shift from "shimmer to solitude." Not a sad kind of solitude, but a recognition that in addition to the romantic who still dwelled in her was this more singular woman who needed time away from people in order to focus on her own creativity, in silence and peace. An outer focus was becoming more inward.

CATCHING WHAT IS FLEETING

WHAT APPEALS to you now doesn't have to be a full-fledged story or someone's new book; it can be just a *glimpse* of some other way of life.

Alec was at a lecture on spirituality given by a Buddhist monk. The speaker defined monk—"monos"—as meaning "alone," with time and energies focused on his practice. Alec sat bolt upright. He had no desire to join the monastery, or even to practice Buddhism, but the word *monk*, with its connotations of an intense, focused energy, reminded him how diffuse and exhausting his life felt. The *character* of this monk in front of him, in his orange robes, got Alec to see a strong desire for change in his life he had been ignoring.

Carol Pearson, who has written extensively on tapping the power of various archetypes (see Resources section), makes the point that the focus in organizational development on "paradigm shifts" reiterates a key fact: All our stories are anachronistic. We all have old, outdated views of who we are. Even as we try to get to a new story, we might tell it in terms of who we have always been.

SOUL MAPPING EXERCISE:

Taking into account your past and present . . . your childhood experiences and your current inclinations, ask yourself:

❧ What is the movie of your life? Write a brief outline of the story of your life, but from another person's perspective. If someone else were to write your story, say your best friend, what would your character be like? What movie are you walking around in? Who would play you in a movie role of your life?

> **HUNTING FOR THE OUTDATED**
>
> *Hint*: The current movie you're living, as well as your interpretation of what you're attracted to you now, may be a type of default mode—the way you are most of the time. That's fine if it works for you now, but often we're trapped in those anachronistic stories we've outgrown. Sometimes the new life pressing us will demand we become a new character. Many of the exercises in this chapter are designed to help you track that emergent energy.

As you read over your responses to the exercises so far, does anything strike you as outdated, or something you have left behind—or want to?

TRAVELING DEEPER:
Charting New Territory

TRACKING THE UNLIVED LIVES

SOMETIMES THE who-you've-always-been sense of yourself keeps you from hearing a new story that is trying to emerge. It may not even get on the radar screen, since there is so much "different" or "other" culture we don't expose ourselves to.

Here are some quick, intuitive ways to brainstorm what may be hoped for, hinted at, ahead of your curve. It takes the above exercises a little further into fantasy. As Robert Johnson put it in *Inner Work*, "Whoever we are, our ego lives are partial systems, with a huge backlog of unlived life hiding within." These exercises help you honor that backlog.

SOUL MAPPING EXERCISE:

- Imagine you're at a cocktail party and have to introduce yourself to people. No one there knows who you really are or what you do, and you won't have to meet any of them again. There are various groups of people standing around, and you decide to introduce yourself to each group as a different person. It could be someone famous (Amelia Earhart, Oprah Winfrey) someone fictional (Tom Sawyer, Clark Kent), or someone whose work you covet (professional athlete, owner of a country inn, novelist, etc.).

- Quickly write down six to eight characters you want to come across as. Here's another way to do this—as a costume party exercise. What six to eight characters would you most like to come to a costume party as?

- Then, write down the salient characteristics of these people. What do they have in common? However farfetched, what do these characters have to say about your longings, talents, hopes, inclinations? How are each of them in some way "true" to you?

The thought of presenting ourselves to total strangers is freeing, because unlike well-meaning friends and family, strangers have no preconceived notions of who we are or what we can or cannot do. Try to imagine yourself in these situations of suspended truth, and see what floats up. Who do you want to become?

CAPTURING YOUR POSITIVE PROJECTIONS

A MORE subtle way to sense who you want to become is to be aware of what figures in the culture you admire. We hear a lot about how we project the things we *don't* like about ourselves onto others; so if someone really bothers you, chances are he or she manifests something you don't like in yourself.

What we hear less about is how the people we like from afar are *also* reflecting parts of ourselves. New possibilities in your life will often come in projected form. Somehow it's safer to see a quality "out there" first. The danger is that we see no connection between who we admire and ourselves, and thus stay stuck in a limited view of ourselves, imbuing the movie or sports star or author or artist with all the "gold" and not taking any of it on ourselves.

Part of the work of this chapter of *Soul Mapping* is uncovering where your soul's energy and excitement gravitate and then reclaiming that energy for your own life. It doesn't mean literally trying to become who you admire, but instead to realize that you couldn't admire that person if you didn't have some of those same qualities yourself. And these figures we put up on pedestals can help point the away; they can show what's just ahead of the curve for us.

Martha was in advertising for many years and not part of any church. In her mid-30s she found herself in a church community she liked, and got involved in parish life. She especially admired the co-pastor, a strong, articulate woman who preached wonderful sermons. As Martha got more involved as a leader herself, she continued to extol this woman, who had become a close friend, and the nature of her work. Martha was surprised when people asked her if she was considering the ministry herself, and noted her gifts for it. She still thought of it as something "special" people did. What people were seeing were her own gifts—even before she could see them.

Martha's soul task here is not to jump into the priesthood necessarily; projections require not imitation but untying: separating out the strands that belong to the person you idealize from the strands you have to claim for yourself. If you keep all the praise heaped on the other, you never have to live out the potential for yourself. Often the best aspects of us become relegated to our "shadow"—the parts of ourselves we refuse to recognize.

SOUL MAPPING EXERCISE: BRAINSTORMING YOUR HEROES AND HEROINES

❧ Write down ten to fifteen people you really admire. They can be famous or not; dead or alive. In another column, write down the characteristics that make you admire that person. What do you notice about these attributes? Are there any themes? Any nudges that you also manifest these qualities . . . or want to?

Julie did this exercise in a counseling session and was embarrassed about some of her results: Mother Teresa, Princess Di, and Oprah Winfrey. But underneath any embarrassment, she was passionate about these women, and about *their* passions to do social service, each in very different ways. In analyzing the attributes of each, Julie realized she too had a desire—and a capacity—to actively be of service, in a visible, public way.

INTERPRETING YOUR CHARACTERS, EXTENDING YOUR STORY

IF THE various exercises so far have floated up a cast of cultural characters, stories and plots, it's important to work with those results, to *extend* them in a way that captures what they mean to you. Just as dream interpretation requires you to bring personal associations to what came to you in the night, this chapter is most useful if you brainstorm what the results might mean, and discern whether or not you are called to act on those results.

SILENCE THE INNER SKEPTIC

Try to not criticize or disown what came up in the exercises. However strange or unlikely something may seem, there are important clues in what you wrote. These clues may be about partial truth: there may be an *aspect* of a life or a story you need to incorporate, not the whole story itself. Try not to react to the new in all-or-nothing ways, thinking it's everything or nothing. This black-and-white thinking makes it all too easy to dismiss our results as mere fantasy.

The best way to search for these clues is to begin by *widening* your interpretation of what has come up for you:

SOUL MAPPING EXERCISE:

> ❧ What are your **personal associations** with the cultural figures and stories that arose? One person's *Gone with the Wind* will mean something very different from someone else's. Why you admire a particular author, actor, athlete, or saint will not be why someone else does. Journal in a wide way for each choice, and let that journaling lead you where it will.

Here's an example of how this method works:

Anne, in her early 40s, was fascinated by the tennis player Martina Hingis. The first time she saw Hingis play, she couldn't stop watching the screen, intrigued by the young woman's style. When she brainstormed her associations with Hingis, she wrote:

> Strong, knowing, athletic, graceful. Also ruthless, powerful, uses racket like a sword. Pitiless, shrewd, clear in her objective. Applies pressure, dominates, moves fast. Single-minded. Takes no prisoners. A warrior. Wins.

When she wrote this, Anne was at a crossroads in her personal life when she especially needed the qualities she attributed to Hingis. Always a "nice," flexible person, Anne needed to tap into her own "warrior" qualities if she was to negotiate her transition successfully. It was important for her to see that she did have access to these "Martina" qualities; she had relegated them to her shadow side, but they were there, waiting to be tapped. Seeing them "out there" in a cultural figure was how the qualities first appeared to her, but they were vague. In the journaling Anne was surprised at how quickly she could name them concretely and specifically. It was as if her soul was just waiting to be asked what it thought. The next step was to integrate what she heard.

RETURNING:
Mapping What You Find, Dreaming the Future

INTEGRATING AND TAKING ACTION

YOU HAVE just spent what we hope has been some fun and surprising time listening for the promptings to your soul hidden in the characters and stories that appeal to you.

Now, as you emerge from this chapter, you need to assess what's come up and apply the "action" question to the results of your personal associations.

Simply put: do you need to take any action in your life, however small, to honor the results of these exercises? (This topic is discussed in detail in the chapter "From Map to Movement.") Not all cultural figures you playfully come up with require any action on your part other than noting them and doing the association work. Others do. To tell the difference, try this exercise:

SOUL MAPPING EXERCISE:

ॐ Look over all the characters, stories and figures that you have come up with in this chapter and ask yourself regarding each one, "Are there any aspects or qualities here that I need to integrate in my life *now*?"

ॐ This integration can work a couple of ways: Perhaps the "movie of your life" exercise produced a story that feels old to you, something you feel trapped in, a role that no longer suits you. The task then is to think of ways to move *out of* that role, to take energy from a new story.

On the other hand if, like Anne in the example above, the energy needed is embodied in the person or story currently capturing you, the task is to move *into* that role somehow, to take on the attributes you need.

Look at all the exercises as possible sources for this integration work. List what comes up:

1. Things I need to move out of:
2. Things I want to move into:

> ## WELCOMING THE NEW
>
> How to integrate and take action around this chapter's potentially "strange" contents? By welcoming that very strangeness!
>
> Jungian psychology points out that it's the unconscious that often initiates the new things in our lives. Because this chapter really taps the power of the unconscious, it's natural that some of the results of the exercises may seem strange. The ego may look at our choices with amazement and the certainty that none of this can be integrated into our "real" life.
>
> It's important not to dismiss the results. Even if a result goes beyond what we feel is possible or appropriate, it is a summons of the soul nonetheless, one we are called to follow in some way.

FOLLOWING THE SUMMONS:
THE POWER OF ACTING SYMBOLICALLY

WE OFTEN don't follow inner promptings because what we see and hear doesn't fit our current sense of ourselves. Or we think following means literal appropriation—we have to *become* that person we're drawn to in some way. Faced with the new thing in our midst, we get stuck and throw up our hands. Integration and action? Impossible.

How to budge from this place of stuckness? By distinguishing a *literal* response from a *symbolic* one. Robert Johnson points out in many of his books that the unconscious doesn't know the difference between doing something actually or symbolically. This is one reason we put such an emphasis on listening to the symbols that arise in your Soul Mapping work. The symbols carry weight and can help you welcome the new.

It's your *personal associations* to the cultural stories and figures you're drawn to that help you decide if and how to integrate them symbolically. It's the associations that provide the bridge from icon out there in the world to some shift you need to make inside.

Without doing the association exercise, Anne, the woman drawn to Martina Hingis, might think she just needed to play more tennis, or watch more of it on television, or she might dismiss her association with Hingis as envy. Her associations revealed the qualities she really needed to draw on at this time in her life.

Tennis, or even ruthlessness, wasn't the literal answer for her. But to see herself as a warrior in her own life, to flex unused muscles of decisiveness and determination, to be more shrewd and a little less friendly—*these* were actions she was called to.

Another Vocare client working on these exercises kept focusing on successful actresses. This did not mean she was supposed to do a mid-career switch and *become* an actress. When she studied which actresses she had picked, they were strong, independent, creative ones in their 40s and 50s whose work was wide-ranging and quirky. Those were precisely the aspects of the work she was trying to find, in a different field.

SOUL MAPPING EXERCISE:

ஐ Look at the people or stories you have come up with in the exercises, especially the ones that seem "impossible" to incorporate into your current life.

ஐ What are your **personal associations** to them? Elaborate on how they are commenting on your life in a way that does fit you now . . . or are summoning you in a way you have a hunch about.

HOLDING THE TENSIONS

TAKING YOUR "summonses" seriously will naturally reveal tensions between the way your life is now and what energies may also be calling you. Alec, the man drawn to the lifestyle of the Buddhist monk, needed to look at the tension between his need for solitude and silence and the demands of his professional and family life. An either/or response would not do. To ignore the inner promptings as impractical, or to abandon the old life and literally become a monk—neither response integrates the tensions; they just embrace one pole or the other.

What Alec did was to carry the powerful picture of a monk as a symbol, a touchstone that reminded him of the daily necessity for some prayer or silent time. For Alec, the routine was crucial; the integration of the monk's message had to show up in not-so-small things like twenty-minute meditation times in solitude; walks during lunch hour instead of eating with a group, etc.

SOUL MAPPING EXERCISE:

- ☙ The tension locator: What tensions naturally arise from your responses to these exercises? Just naming them, bringing them to the surface, helps.
- ☙ What can you do to live creatively with the tension—not banish it? Can you carry an image or symbol of what the tension represents? Can you speak about it with someone, pray over it, journal further about it? In essence, live with it as creatively as you can and continue to receive the wisdom it brings.

VOCATION LURKS HERE, TOO

KEEP AN eye out in your responses for vocational clues. The results of the heroes and heroines exercise can often point toward your own vocational gifts, as does the cocktail party exercise. They can reveal literal directions you might want to explore, as well as symbolic clues.

SOUL MAPPING EXERCISE:

- ☙ What do your responses say about your gifts? What has been there all along? What's trying to emerge?
- ☙ If you currently are not happy doing what you do, what are the missing elements? What energy or embodiment is needed?
- ☙ Are there cultural figures associated with what you really want to do now—what you yearn to do? Someone in news, politics, the arts, education, ministry, etc.? If you were to align yourself symbolically with this figure, would you learn something about your own embodied traits in the area you yearn for?

WATCH YOUR CULTURAL DIET

WHILE THIS chapter celebrates the way culture can carry clues for our soul work, it's still important to watch what we take in. The images we "eat" are powerful, as important as the food we eat. Many spiritual practices advocate a "news fast"— going without newspapers and television as a way to clear the mind. With the Internet, it's even more tempting to be awash in images and information.

Carl Jung once commented that "We can only suffer a certain amount of culture without injury." Balance is key: Listen to popular culture for the clues to your own unconscious it can provide; at the same time, don't let it overload you.

FINAL NOTE: HONOR THE LIVING WATER

IMAGINE YOURSELF as a deep well. Stories give us a way to bring the hidden, living water up to the surface. If we seal ourselves off from this water, the well dries up from disuse. Our sense of what is possible for ourselves shrinks. Stories in our culture tap into our wells of experience and longing.

The powerful patterns that appeal to us from the culture break into our consciousness in all sorts of ways. We have used various exercises to encourage that breaking in. Ultimately, this work is not about conforming to culture. The goal is what author and Jungian analyst Ann Ulanov calls in her lectures "the revolutionary idea of breaking through to your own preferences." The stories we're drawn to are just pointing the way.

Look at what you have pulled up in this section of your Soul Map. How is it both a *description* and a *prescription* for you?

Now turn to the Circle Page to capture the most important information from this chapter.

Circle Page Questions

⤜ ✺ ⤛

Your Circle Page:
What "Angels Are Knocking?"

LOOK OVER all you have written for this chapter. Think of it as a particular journey unto itself, into very specific territory. You return from this exploration with many thoughts and impressions. As a way to start that honing and honoring process, answer these questions quickly and intuitively. You can write directly in your circle or answer the questions on another piece of paper and then transfer the results to the Circle Page. Either way, this is a place to record the most insistent (and possibly most important) data from your responses; a place to capture the "angels knocking" at your door.

- What main stories and themes came up as emblematic of your life?
- What shifts did you spot between stories you identified with in your past and stories you identify with now?
- What are the most appealing, powerful "unlived lives" that beckon to you? How might you incorporate them into your current life?
- What positive qualities do you most often project onto other people?
- What are the main tensions between the characters or stories you came up with in this chapter? How can you hold those tensions creatively?

SACRED PLACE

OF ALL the answers to exercises in this chapter, which one(s) feel most sacred and important to you at this time in your life?

EMOTION

IS THERE a predominant emotion in your responses to the exercises?

SURPRISE

WHAT MOST surprised you about your responses in this chapter? What do you know now that you did not know before?

NURTURE AND RENEWAL

WHICH ANSWERS spoke the most to a hunger or a longing? Is there an aspect of your answers that, if it were more integrated in your life right now, would be particularly nurturing and helpful to you?

PERSONAL IMPERATIVE

AS YOU review your answers to this chapter, do you sense any imperative arising from what you wrote—any need to change your life? If so, where is the urge for change most insistent in this chapter?

THE POWER OF PLACE
FAVORITE TRAVELS AND INNER TERRAINS

"The whole of life of a person

is the slow trek to recover the

two or three simple images in whose

presence his heart first moved."

—Albert Camus

GETTING THE LAY OF THE LAND

A WEBSTER'S dictionary defines "traveler" as "one who explores regions more or less unknown." That definition is at the heart of the Soul Mapping process, since readers travel though various layers of a topic, often for the first time. Through exercises, the known mixes with the unknown; the soul makes itself heard; ideas for future action emerge.

Travel and exploration are important enough themes in Soul Mapping to warrant a chapter all their own. Since people are navigating the shifts of their inner geography in creating their Soul Map, it's important to give a place to literal geography, and the sheer power of place.

We all have a map of places in our mind—of places that we would like to go.

This chapter is not an exercise in teasing or frustrating those with limited travel budgets. It asks: What do those places of instant rapport or longing tell us about ourselves? Why *this* country and not *that* one? How does our affinity for one type of landscape reveal itself in other areas of our life? Is there something we need to do to "accommodate" that geographic pull? We have lots of "landscapes" existing within us; this chapter will help you discover and work with them.

The utterly concrete qualities of geography make it a preferred medium of the soul. The smell of the ocean, the feel of pine needles underfoot, a mountain range in the distance, the energy of a city street: Our souls connect with landscape in visceral, non-verbal ways. Our preferences in travel—and our attitude toward it—hold many clues pertinent to the Soul Mapping process.

One key to this chapter is to have fun with it. While that is true of all the chapters in this book, being playful as you do this chapter allows you to not be hemmed in by literal requisites of travel: cost, distance, time off. Even as an "armchair traveler" you can have a powerful experience with this chapter. Feel free to take off with it, dream with it, let the soul speak through it.

LIFE AS A JOURNEY

ONE OF our assumptions in writing this chapter is that everyone "travels": whether literally to different countries, or as a journeyer in their own life as it unfolds. How that looks can take many forms; mountain climbing is not required. A naturalist once described his travel plans for the three-month summer vacation: He would move his chair, inch-by-inch, across his backyard, while he studied each blade of grass. That was it. For him, this was a deep, meticulous and refreshing exploration he had never had time for. What travel beckons to you? It may be very near.

The travel we all do also includes detours and suffering. The whole concept of the "hero's journey" links journeying with development of human character. Typically, adventurers set out in search of something or to conquer something. Usually the hero is tested. He or she finds himself in difficult circumstances that require wit and cunning to evade or escape. Experience along the way adds to skill and a sense of how the world works. Suffering usually accompanies this learning process, and the hero learns just by going through things persistently.

Inching along the grass in the suburban backyard? Going forth like Odysseus and having adventures? The terrain—inner and outer—is potent in both.

TRAVEL AS A THRESHOLD MOMENT

AS YOU do the exercises in this chapter, pause to reflect on one way travel fascinates: It takes us into new space that is not predetermined. It shakes up the routine of our existence and gives us new perspective. When you voyage somewhere new, nobody knows you there. No well-meaning friends or family have a sense of what you can do and can't do, what you like or don't like. You may look at new places you travel to with fresh eyes, and that's exactly how the new places and people are looking at *you*: no preconceived notions, no assumptions.

In this way, travel is about threshold and liminal space: you are between identities, suspended between what you have temporarily left behind and what you will glean from where you are going. In this space the soul can speak through new sights and smells, different rhythms, languages and cultures. You're open and the new place is open to you. Invoke that sense of spaciousness and openness to surprise as you do this chapter's exercises.

BEGINNING EXPLORATIONS:
Surveying the Past and the Present

WHAT KIND OF TRAVELER ARE YOU?

THIS CHAPTER blends brainstorming and daydreaming about literal landscapes with some questions about attitude. As a child, you didn't have much choice about how and when you traveled, but as an adult, it's your call. Yet despite the seeming freedom to approach travel any way we want, we come at the idea of it with baggage, as it were. Some ways to identify yours:

SOUL MAPPING EXERCISE:

- ✑ How do you view travel in general? Eagerly? Gingerly? Skeptically? Routinely? Longingly?
- ✑ Let travel assume some of its metaphoric power: Since it is often about movement, and newness, and uncertainty and maybe even envy, how do you approach it? What role does it have in your life?

❧ Do you think of yourself as a "traveler?" If so, why? Where are you traveling to? If not, why not?

❧ Who are you traveling with? Do you travel alone? If travel is in part about growth and newness, who are the people or communities in your life you explore with? That exploration could have nothing to do with getting on airplanes and everything to do with inner work. Who or what in your life encourages you to travel deeply?

❧ Who are the most important current travelers with you on your path?

❧ How might you add some helpful fellow travelers to your circle of people at this time in your life?

CHILDHOOD TRAVELS AND LANDSCAPES

THINK BACK to what it was like to travel as a child in your family. There can be lots of rich associations from our first experiences outside the territory we called home.

SOUL MAPPING EXERCISE:

❧ How did your parents view travel, and how does that compare with how you view it today? Did they think it was risky, expensive, essential, hard, exciting? What landscapes did they love? Did they go to them?

❧ Where did you go as a family? What did you do? Was it a happy time or a tense time? What associations do you have with childhood travel?

❧ What were your favorite childhood landscapes? What kinds of environments do you feel most connected and content in? As you write your responses, see if you can also draw and color them, or cut out magazine pictures that remind you of places you loved as a child. Include photos from family albums.

❧ How did you travel as an adolescent? Did you travel, however temporarily, as a way to "leave home?"

❧ What travels do you wish you had made as a teenager or young adult?

TRAVELING DEEPER:
Charting New Territory

As we travel, whether across town or across the world, we are certain types of explorers: shaped by past travel experiences or the lack of them; longing for certain landscapes; planning or not planning the voyage, depending on our temperament. Do we set out with a clear itinerary, or are we charmed by detours and diversions? Are we traveling for curiosity's sake, or because of some deep longing that is hard to articulate, even to ourselves?

HONING IN ON OUR "HOME PORT"

In the previous section of this chapter, you brought to mind some early associations with travel. Whatever your method as a traveler, one of our assumptions is that the soul is always trying to head for some sort of "home port." That place of belonging can naturally shift over time, or can remain centered around a natural element, like water or open sky. As you continue with this section's exercises, keep this "home port" idea in mind; see where the geographic hunger is, and what it might be saying. We will include lots of ways to help you tease this out.

LANDSCAPE HUNGER

Close your eyes and think about the landscapes that feed your soul deeply. These may be places you are familiar with, or have always wanted to see.

Dick describes this power of place: "A woman I knew years ago was absolutely addicted to the ocean. She would go there all year round, even on the coldest weekends. And in the spring when the water was still very cold, she would jump and play in the surf as long as she could. Then the summer found her totally immersed, treading water for hours like some primordial fish. She told me once that all her life she had lived on the surface of things, and that in the last few years, as she plunged more and more into the sea, there was the parallel discovery of the deep places in herself."

SOUL MAPPING EXERCISE:

- ❧ What is your favorite place? What does it look like? Where are you most comfortable?
- ❧ What landscapes make you the most uncomfortable, and are the ones you most want to avoid?
- ❧ Are there any shifts between places you were once drawn to and places that capture you now?
- ❧ If you had a free week to rest anywhere, where would it be? What landscape would surround you?
- ❧ Where do you dream of moving to? Why?

TRACKING CULTURAL RESONANCE

SPECIFIC PLACES may be both powerful for us and accessible, like the ocean was for the woman DICK knew. But "Favorite Travels and Inner Terrains" also encompasses different cultures, even ones we have never experienced firsthand. Just as the soul can say something insistent and important through books, movies and characters we are attracted to, different lands and cultures also hold clues to who we need to become.

One friend we know fell in love with Italy and in one trip there, brought it back with her in many ways. She has not yet returned, but she *lives* it in some interesting ways right here in New York City. She savors her red wine; she makes the time to make risotto. With a certain *brio* she finally switched to a much better job after many years of being stuck. Coincidence? We don't think so.

DICK describes the fascination Spain has for him: "For many years now I have spent much time exploring the music, the art, and the cuisine of Spain. Something about it beckoned to me. Perhaps it is my combination Germanic and English soul that longs for some Mediterranean spice and vigor. I don't know, but I knew I wanted to go there. I was thirsty and hungry for it. And the experience of going there was wonderful, the perfect mixture of preparation and love. Even upon return I continue my study and deepening of my understanding of this great people and the place where they live. I could do this for many other regions as well. They resonate in my soul, feed me, and give me life."

At one point in her career NINA did a lot of work as a promotional writer for the French Government Tourist Office. "Looking back, this was a mysterious time

I still don't quite understand. I didn't speak French that well, and I hadn't been to the places I was describing. But I was utterly absorbed by the geography in this country, and by the romantic aura I ascribed to the whole place. I researched towns exhaustively, wrote copy that tried to capture what I felt was sublime about these beautiful, compelling places. When I went there and wandered, it was like being a pilgrim in a holy land. The connection was visceral, and fed a hunger I didn't know I had. That connection has faded now, but I will never forget the sense of being wedded to places I had not even been to. This was a soul connection, though I did not know it at the time, or have the language to communicate it. Nor could I see how the need for France commented on what was missing at home, in my life in New York. In retrospect, I can make the connection."

SOUL MAPPING EXERCISE:

- ❧ What cultures fascinate you and why? What music and food inspire you?
- ❧ What do these attractions say about you? About what is currently missing from your life . . . or an aspect of your personality you want to encourage?
- ❧ Have you shifted in your life in terms of what cultures you are drawn to?
- ❧ How can you integrate aspects of these cultures that attract you into your life now?

YOUR SACRED SPACES

IN THE section before, Italy, Spain, and France all had qualities of the sacred for the people who experienced them. There was a mysterious, compelling, life-giving aspect to these places. That quality can call us from different spaces at different times in our lives. It's important to the Soul Mapping process to have sacred places you can rely on, spend time in, be nourished by. The word "sacred" comes from the Greek word for "safe," which captures it perfectly: Think about the safe spaces that hold you and speak to your soul particularly. They may be connected with a church or religious sanctuary, they may be in nature, or they may have roots in your childhood.

Sacred spaces can be places in the memory that have special significance for us, and that continue to play out in our lives, in different incarnations. DICK remembers: "When I was a young boy, I was the gang leader of a small marauding band of troublemakers. We built several places in the woods, which were our camps. And from these outposts we led attacks on various other gangs of kids, hatched schemes of possible and impossible proportions, and generally learned about one another and how to get along. Some of the places were made for talking, some for lookout, and some for storing our stuff.

I realize today, as I lead a counseling center in my community, that I am repeating much of the terrain I traversed back in those days of yore. My staff is the gang, our counseling rooms are the camps, and we often sit around hatching schemes for the future direction of the center. I realize that these spaces are very important to me and always have been. I want them to be roomy, beautiful, and functional. I want them to have rooms, and toys, and meaning, which they do."

NAMING YOUR SACRED SPACES

Look back over all the "terrains" you have experienced or dreamed of in your life. What are the most compelling ones for you; the ones that could be called sacred? Draw them . . . find pictures of them in magazines . . . look at old photo albums.

How have your sacred spaces shifted over time? Which do you most want to be in contact with now? What can you to evoke them on a regular basis?

SOUL CONNECTION: ENTER THE IRRATIONAL

USUALLY A soulful, indicative connection with a place has roots in our past, evolves from our work, or hooks up with some aspect of our lives. But not always. This is a time to do some quick, intuitive exercises around the power of place. The questions go beyond asking about a culture that attracts or a sacred spot. Put practicality aside, take pencil in hand, close your eyes, take a deep breath, and ask yourself:

SOUL MAPPING EXERCISE:

❧ What places do you feel you are "supposed" to go to? Places where there is some compelling pull or attraction? What does this imply about you?

❧ Write down the first thing that comes to mind: If you were to escape your life, where in the world would you escape to?

❧ If your ability to travel ended tomorrow, where would you most regret not visiting? Be as specific as you can and list as many places as you can.

❧ Do you associate any places or landscapes with healing and serenity? Again, be specific.

RETURNING:
Mapping What You Find, Dreaming the Future

THIS IS a chapter where what you "return" with from your exercises tells you a lot about where you may need to go. Mapping this section of your Soul Map can be evocative, compelling, even frustrating, if the exotic travel longings are all taken literally.

Travel is about curiosity, and longing, and belonging. Doing these exercises is a way to listen deeply for the landscapes your soul desires. As a result, dreaming the future can mean making travel plans—it can also mean tracing patterns, integrating aspects of what you have uncovered, and re-thinking how you approach exploration.

TRACING YOUR TRAVEL PATTERN

THERE ARE dual tracks in this chapter: the travel you have done and want to do, and the overall journey aspects of your life. Even if we never leave our home town, we are going somewhere in our lives. And whether this direction arises from an inward intuitive sense, or comes from the outside like the force of fate, there is a definite pattern. Many of us look back on our lives, and what seemed confusing and wrong often has the look of a pattern about it. In a sense what had seemed to be a crazy quilt has turned into a beautiful tapestry.

Look back over your answers so far and ask yourself:

SOUL MAPPING EXERCISE:

❧ What are you focused on in your current journey?

❧ Where are you going? Like Odysseus, where is the home you're trying to get to, and what distracts you from getting there?

- What or where is your "true north"? Your home port?
- Is your journey too planned, or not planned enough? Anything you would change about that?
- Carl Jung once said that "The right way to wholeness is through fitful starts and wrong turnings." Do you have enough "wrong turnings" to get you to the place you need to get to?

TRAVEL AS MIRROR: WHAT NEEDS TO CHANGE?

CONTINUING WITH the theme of our life as a journey, our attitudes toward travel act as all-too-accurate mirrors of how we approach living. NINA recalls: "My best friend Kate dazzled me with her abilities to travel, starting as a teenager. She had no qualms about going to Europe alone, exploring and working there. I traveled about fifty miles for summer vacation; she crossed the Atlantic. I couldn't imagine doing this. Even when she had a job for two years in Monaco in her 20s, and begged me to visit, I put it off, waiting for the 'right' time to make such a big maiden voyage. Of course, that *was* the right moment, and I regret not visiting her to this day. We laugh about it now, and she forgave me my timidity, but looking back I can see how this hesitation and this tendency to make something loom larger than it really is lurks a little too powerfully in other areas of my life as an adult."

SOUL MAPPING EXERCISE:

- How does your profile as a traveler reflect how you are in other areas of your life? Are you cautious? Bold and impulsive? Curious? Nervous?
- Is there anything you want to change about the above?
- Is there anything that will have to change in order to incorporate more of the landscapes you long for into your life?

INTEGRATING THE LONGED-FOR LANDSCAPES

THE LANDSCAPES you long for . . . the cultures that attract . . . your soul offers these up to you in this chapter, and can be satisfied in many ways. Think of the variety of ways you can integrate the energies of the places that are most powerful for you.

SOUL MAPPING EXERCISE:

❧ Where do you most need to go? What literal travel needs to be planned for now and looked forward to now?

❧ Is there something you need to do to "accommodate" the geographic pulls you have articulated in these exercises? For instance, can you incorporate aspects of a culture that attracts you by exploring the cuisine, the literature, the music?

❧ What nearby travel is at hand to nourish you? Parks, churches, monasteries, lakes, etc.?

❧ Are there any opposites that tug at you from the results of your exercises? Are you land-locked and longing for water? Quiet and shy and wanting the fire of a Latin culture? On flat plains and dreaming of mountains? In a city and hungry for open sky? Think of what these desires might mean both literally and metaphorically. Is there a part of your personality that needs to come out whether you travel to these potent places or not?

❧ Finally, is there a place calling you out of your current surroundings? Are you at a make or break point vis à vis your work and where you live? At a crucial point in her career, painter Georgia O'Keefe knew she had to leave the green mountains of the East Coast, and go to the Southwest, where large, open spaces fit her shifting artistic vision. Do you feel you need to live in a certain place in order to become who you want to become? Is there a way you can explore or plan for or just do this?

YOUR TRAVEL TOKENS

Look over all the places and landscapes that came up for you in this chapter. Even if can't visit them anytime soon, think of creating a space on your Soul Map—and also in your home—to remind you of the energy and promise these places hold for you. Pay particular attention if you were surprised by something that came up: You don't have to visit a place to start to explore what it means for you at this time in your life.

Find pictures and brochures of the place; cut out pleasing images and keep them visible. Use the Internet to research travel to these places. Imagine the place as an integral part of your psyche—because it is.

"LIVING LIVE OF EXPLORATION"

T.S. ELIOT has written that our lives are comprised of ceaseless exploration, and that we often arrive where we started, except we now know the place—and perhaps ourselves—for the first time. The cyclical nature of the voyaging he describes captures the paradox—and the blessing—of our travels: that it is in setting out that we eventually find our true home; that we travel in a circle, not a straight line. The process can take years, but at last it combines the unknown so inherent in travel with a sense of profound arrival. That sense of belonging—to our own lives, to our own souls—only comes from brave voyages both inner and outer. May this chapter hold both familiar and provocative guideposts for you as you journey.

CIRCLE PAGE QUESTIONS

——— ❧ ———

YOUR CIRCLE PAGE:
What "Angels Are Knocking?"

LOOK OVER all you have written for this chapter. Think of it as a particular journey unto itself, into very specific territory. You return from this exploration with many thoughts and impressions. As a way to start that honing and honoring process, answer these questions quickly and intuitively. You can write directly in your circle or answer the questions on another piece of paper and then transfer the results to the Circle Page. Either way, this is a place to record the most insistent (and possibly most important) data from your responses; a place to capture the "angels knocking" at your door.

- What cultures or landscape most draw you today? What favorite places beckon to you?
- What kind of travel—inner or outer—do you want to incorporate into your life today?
- Where is your "true north"?
- Have you thought of your own life as a journey? What are some of the themes?
- Where are you headed?

SACRED PLACE

OF ALL the answers to exercises in this chapter, which one(s) feel most sacred and important to you at this time in your life?

EMOTION

IS THERE a predominant emotion in your responses to the exercises?

SURPRISE

WHAT MOST surprised you about your responses in this chapter? What do you know now that you did not know before?

NURTURE AND RENEWAL

WHICH ANSWERS spoke the most to a hunger or a longing? Is there an aspect of your answers that, if it were more integrated in your life right now, would be particularly nurturing and helpful to you?

PERSONAL IMPERATIVE

AS YOU review your answers to this chapter, do you sense any imperative arising from what you wrote—any need to change your life? If so, where is the urge for change most insistent in this chapter?

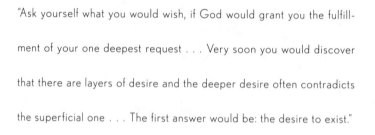

7

THE ENERGY OF ENVY
WHO YOU COVET AND WHY

———— ❧ ————

"Ask yourself what you would wish, if God would grant you the fulfill-

ment of your one deepest request . . . Very soon you would discover

that there are layers of desire and the deeper desire often contradicts

the superficial one . . . The first answer would be: the desire to exist."

—Fritz Kunkel, quoted in *The Choice Is Always Ours*

GETTING THE LAY OF THE LAND

Yes, ENVY has its reputation as one of the "seven deadly sins." Why should we devote a whole chapter to it? Because envy can be a wonderful "back door" into desire and the true self. It's a mirror into our own lives and aspirations that allows us to see things and admit things initially. As a form of peripheral vision, it's often the first place where desires, clues, and aspirations appear. If left unexamined, these aspirations can stay in the form of projection onto others, who forever do the things we would like to—while we stay simmering in our envy. That angry, stuck place is deadly indeed. But to use envy as an energy locator, as a way to listen to the soul and move *beyond* being stuck, is a whole other way of working with this ancient, basic, primal emotion we all have.

People describe themselves as being "green" with envy. It's interesting that the color green denotes both sickness and growth. And like that color, envy can lead us to both sickness or to genuine change and renewal.

Envy is a powerful force in our life that can be used for insight and growth if we can enter into a deep listening process and honestly admit our longings and desires. The goal of this chapter is to get you to experience your feelings of envy and identify the people and qualities you most envy. The exercises will help you acknowledge your hidden or not-so-hidden feelings of envy. Understanding the sources of your envy and creatively translating your longings into real life goals appropriate to you then becomes an exciting adventure and a vital part of the Soul Mapping process.

ENVY AS SHADOW MATERIAL

As we mentioned in the chapter on "Culture that Captures," Carl Jung coined the term "shadow" to refer to the repudiated, disowned parts and potentials of the self. The shadow can contain positive things about ourselves we refuse to see, as well as the things we think are negative or "wrong." Envy, with all its undercurrents, is prime shadow material. By entering into your envious feelings and honestly recalling and coming to terms with them, you can give yourself a window into your personal "shadow." This perspective can help you begin a process of growth by helping you reclaim and reappropriate aspects of yourself.

Envy is our wanting those qualities we see in another person. An anonymous quote describes envy as "admiration tinged with despair." In this way envy also carries within it resentment toward the other person and a belief that we can never possess what he or she has—hence the despair. This darker side of envy can keep us in an angry, stuck position.

ENVY AS A TOOL FOR CHANGE

IF ENVY just helped you locate where you were truly mired, it wouldn't be much of a Soul Mapping tool! But we are asking you to take envy one freeing step further: The exercises in this chapter ask you to let go of one stubborn envy assumption—that you can never possess the qualities you envy.

Our hypothesis is exactly the opposite—that the qualities you envy in the other person are often the very qualities that need to be born in you. In fact, the qualities we repudiate or stifle in ourselves are the same as those we see and envy in others. So taking a serious look at your envy—an inventory of it—can be a valuable way to detect your true longings and unfulfilled potential. By teaching you the value of envy and of first identifying and then taking these projections back, you can get glimpses of directions you might want to head in.

BEGINNING EXPLORATIONS:
Surveying the Past and the Present

"BUT WE DON'T DO ENVY"

MANY OF us have been taught since childhood that envy—like anger, fear, jealousy and certain other emotions—is bad and unacceptable. Often as a consequence of family values, we have simply suppressed any sense of envy or of wanting something another person possesses.

KEN remembers: "My father almost never expressed envious or desirous thoughts. In fact, he was the kind of man for whom it was difficult to buy a birthday or Christmas gift. He would never tell you what he wanted! The only expressions of envy I ever recall hearing from him were indirect. As we drove past the homes of the wealthiest people in our town, he would sigh and say 'That doctor is pretty well fixed.' His envy came out indirectly."

NINA reports that with clients, envy is often either the most difficult or the most enjoyable part of the Soul Map they work on. "Many people start with the assumption that I am asking them to reveal "bad" things about themselves in the envy section. That it will prove they are nasty, or petty in some way. So I make sure to emphasize the non-judgmental, freeing, energy-locating qualities of this section. Either people do very skimpy work in this section, or they give themselves permission to really listen within, and it's the most rich."

Despite our efforts to suppress envious thoughts, they do tend to come out indirectly. This is because *we all have envious thoughts*. By giving yourself permission to feel and think envy, you can begin to tap into a new source of guidance and direction.

A note on that source of guidance: The envy we're speaking of is different than cultural materialism, though we realize it can be hard to untangle which envy urges are materialistic, and which are not. And of course, some of what we long for in other people's lives may have to do with material objects, or financial security.

Here's the distinction: The envy we're speaking of may have materialistic components, but it doesn't end there. It will probably also be about attributes and qualities that aren't just financial. In addition to getting beyond the sense that "we don't do envy," allow yourself in these exercises to get beyond trappings and into aspects of character and philosophy.

LOCATING PRESENT ENVY ENERGY: DO AN "ENVY DAY"

AS A way to get more "direct" with the emotion that is usually so indirect, we invite you to spend an entire day tapping into envy. Do this playfully; it's not supposed to raise blood pressure, but awareness. It calls to consciousness thoughts that probably occur each day anyway, underneath the surface.

SOUL MAPPING EXERCISE

- ☙ Spend a whole day looking for your current envious feelings as you encounter colleagues, friends and family. Extend the search to the media: books, television, newspapers, etc. Jot down the feelings as you have them.

- ☙ At the end of the day, list some of the people you envy: the friends, colleagues, media figures, etc. you came up with. Next to each name, write the qualities or circumstances about them that you envy. Hold on to your results; we will come back to your list later in the chapter.

LET IMAGES GRAB YOU

The "envy day" exercise lends itself perfectly to cutting out pictures from glossy magazines. Look for images that capture the qualities or circumstances you associate with the people that came up on your list.

Envy in the family

OF ALL the groups in which envy abounds, the family is the most influential and basic. We see envy between siblings. We see it between husband and wife, and we see it in the various parent/child pairings that go on throughout the history of any family.

For children, what is most desired in the family is the love of the parent. If one child senses an imbalance of love, he or she blames the rival "beloved" sibling. KEN remembers how their oldest daughter Kirsten, at age three, suggested to her parents that they now return her brother to the hospital. She had had enough competition for love.

We also see a child bonding with one parent and wanting to exclude the other parent. Freud described this as the classical Oedipal triangle. KEN: "Our youngest daughter, Amanda, also at age three, once whispered to me the suggestion that she and I run away, move to Disney World, and live happily ever after. Clearly, we were to be together forever, without the interference and competition of other family members, including my wife."

Sometimes envy is a result of families defining or assigning simplistic characteristics to particular children, such as "Bonnie is the smart one," "Bill is the athletic one," "Sherry is the cute one," and so on. This may be an unconscious way of dividing characteristics to avoid competition and envy, yet it has the unintended consequence of limiting people's self-definitions.

Through such characterizations and classifications, family members come to genuinely believe that they are "X" and not "Y." The qualities they are told they do not have are often the qualities they secretly envy.

In the process of counseling clients, we have discovered that these family beliefs and messages are most often inaccurate. Once people begin to question their family descriptions, they can claim for themselves the characteristics which they envy.

SOUL MAPPING EXERCISE:

> ✒ Has there been anyone in your nuclear or extended family whom you envy? List them. Describes the qualities they embody which you envy.

ৰ Can you claim these qualities, or variations of these qualities, for yourself? How would you go about doing that?

ৰ Describe your reputation in your family, using this sentence "You are the _____ one who always _____."

ৰ In what ways has your family's definition of you been limiting?

ৰ What are some ways you might entertain a more expansive self definition? What behavioral risks could you take that someone in your family might describe as "not like you at all"?

ENVY IN OUR WORLD

BEYOND THE family, each of us can surely point to people we have envied in the past. Perhaps that girl in the fifth grade who seemed so perfect. Or maybe that high school athlete so popular with girls. Or the person in college who won all the writing contests. What about your first years at work? Who inspired envy?

Here again is an opportunity to tap into our envy from the past in order to divine the qualities we may have longed for then and that still have a role to play in our lives today.

SOUL MAPPING EXERCISE:

ৰ Do an "envy scan" of various times in your life. This is similar to the "envy day" exercise, except it asks you to look at various stages of your past.

ৰ Review the following periods of your life:

> Childhood, birth to age 10
> Adolescence, ages 10-18
> Young adulthood, ages 18-30

ৰ From each period, choose one or two people you envied who are non-family members. They might be peers, mentors or figures from the popular culture. Take some time to build your list of people whom you envied.

ৰ After you have done this, ask yourself these questions about each person: What was it about this person that you so envied? What qualities or characteristics?

❧ Having done this with three to six people, look over your answers. What patterns do you
see? Were there any common qualities? If so, list them and elaborate on those qualities.
Perhaps you will see a recurrent theme, such as freedom, affluence, wit or self-confidence.

TRAVELING DEEPER:
Charting New Territory

TAKING ALL the riches of the previous envy exercises, we now want you to voyage a little deeper with them. While it's important to discern the qualities you wished or wish for, it's just as important to translate these qualities into realistic, appropriate possibilities for yourself.

> **APPROPRIATE, NOT IMITATE**
>
> Hint: Translating feelings of envy into action is not about imitation. Certain qualities appeal to you for reasons having to do with *you*, not the person envied. The key is to notice the energy and the clues as they first appear outside, in someone else, and then think about ways you can incorporate those qualities in your own, unique ways. As a result, these qualities could end up looking very different in your life than when you first spied them in someone else's.

TRANSLATING YOUR ENVY

REVIEW THE results of this chapter's exercises and look for traits and qualities at the heart of the envy. Now begins the work of translating the traits you envied into a possible, attainable vision for yourself.

SOUL MAPPING EXERCISE:

❧ What would the traits you envied look like in you?

❧ What steps are necessary for you to reach these goals?

ɜ‍ What would be some behavioral indicators or patterns you'd have to adopt if you were to incorporate or embody those qualities?

ɜ‍ Take the time to share these thoughts and stories with a trusted friend. Describe your thoughts and intentions. Sharing your story with a trusted companion is yet another way of anchoring your intentions and making your thoughts and plans real.

WHAT ABOUT GETTING STUCK?

IN THE previous exercise, we asked you to look traits and qualities, not just cir-cumstances. It's when we focus too much on the circumstances—very rich lifestyle, etc.—that we can get stuck in this translating process, thinking, "Well, I don't have a lot of money, so . . . this is useless. I'll never be like that."

Our approach to envy holds that many people get stuck, unable to creatively incorporate their envy qualities into their lives. We're so imbued by our culture to assume that envied qualities are impossible for us to have that it is difficult for us to translate these qualities into our lives. We can be too literal about the trans-lating, or too ambitious in the changes we feel have to happen for anything to be incorporated. When you get stuck this way, try to persevere, because beyond the wall of seeming impossibility may lie a breakthrough.

KEN went through just such an impasse in this translating exercise recently:

"I had something of a revelation in this area. While helping participants in our Soul Mapping workshops identify the sources of their envy, I became aware of how much I envied my friend and collaborator, Richard Shoup. So I went on to ask the pertinent questions.

"What qualities and characteristics was I envying in DICK? And here were my answers:

His lifestyle.

His freedom from family constraints.

His free time and discretionary time.

His assets and freedom from responsibilities.

"Up to that point, this exercise was relatively easy for me. It was when I got to the translation question—How can I translate these qualities into my life?—that the process became difficult.

"I hit a roadblock. My life is very different from DICK's. My wife and I have three children, numerous expenses, no family assets and not much free time. So my first answer to the question of how I could incorporate DICK's envied characteristics was: No way! I just can't incorporate any of these qualities.

"But then I gave it some more time and new possibilities emerged. It gradually dawned on the me that I really do desire more free time for creative pursuits. I began to think of ways to carve out some personal time for creativity. I considered signing up for a drawing class on Tuesday evenings. I thought of blocking out time on Fridays for personal reflection and exercise. As I was thinking about this, a sense of relief and exhilaration came upon me. I *could* incorporate some of the qualities I envied in DICK.

"Even though my life situation is entirely different from my friend's, there were elements I could translate if I made a creative and determined effort to do so. So often, we tend to view ourselves as stuck in a lifestyle or responsibilities that are unchangeable and non-negotiable. Yet so often, the assumptions that change is not possible are merely self-imposed beliefs, not realities."

That's why it is so important to question our assumptions about work, family responsibilities, money, etc. More is possible than we at first may think.

SOUL MAPPING EXERCISE:

Look back over your initial responses to the "Translating your envy" exercise.

❧ Do you see any additions you want to make to our answers?

❧ Look for places where you feel "stuck" in your answers: traits you want to take on, changes you want to make, but it all feels "impossible" or simply too hard. Just as KEN modified his adaptation of aspects of DICK's life in ways that worked for him, are there *small steps* you can take to start the appropriation process? List them here.

EMBODYING THE QUALITIES WE ENVY

ONE WAY to appropriate qualities we envy is through embodiment—a powerful way of incorporating these new qualities and disrupting old patterns by "acting as if."

John Wesley, the Methodist theologian and founder of the Methodist church, once said "We preach faith until we have it." In a similar way, Alcoholics Anonymous members talk about "as if" thinking, through which they make changes by acting as if the changes have already occurred.

Even though we may lack the needed confidence, strength, or resolve in a certain area, we can still act "as if" until the quality we seek becomes a part of us.

KEN: "I remember a client of mine many years ago who was experiencing a very troubling difficulty in his social life. He was very shy around women. But at the same time, he wanted very much to have a relationship. He found that shyness prevented him from introducing himself or even entering into situations where he might meet some new people.

"As we continued to talk about his issues surrounding shyness, we found ourselves discussing questions of movie characters, acting and similar topics. And he explained he was a big fan of Clint Eastwood. I jumped on this as a possible exercise: Why couldn't he *pretend* to be Clint Eastwood, embody those qualities of quiet and reserve, but at the same time appropriate qualities of power and confidence? We explored the character of Clint Eastwood, particularly in his Westerns. The quiet, powerful man who would enter a room with great confidence. My client began to get into this "game" and see it as a useful, transitional step for his own ability to meet people and to move with more confidence in two social settings.

"Two weeks after we discovered the possibility of the Clint Eastwood game, my client came into my office with a western hat on, covering his receding hairline, and sat down without a word. But he seemed to suddenly embody a kind of confident demeanor. We continued to talk with some humor about his Clint Eastwood persona and how it had already helped them meet several women and even go on several dates. This persona and this "as if" pattern assisted him in finding inner confidence and achieving his own personal goals."

SOUL MAPPING EXERCISE:

- ❧ Is there a quality in someone you envy that you could see yourself safely embodying?
- ❧ What steps could you take to embody that quality?

SIFTING THROUGH MATERIALISTIC LONGINGS

EMBODYING IS a powerful and transitional strategy for incorporating internal qualities. Of course, this approach doesn't work for issues of money, fame, material wealth or other external desires. When applied to these desires, this approach may cause us to simply appear to be phony pretenders. However, our desires for external trappings are nonetheless clues in themselves.

We have seen in our Soul Mapping work that materialistic, external desires are often a veneer covering deeper longings for serenity, self-confidence, or better connections with other people. It's important to go deeper in discerning the soul's message in your envy qualities. This is particularly true if you harbor many materialistic, external desires. The following exercise can help you.

SOUL MAPPING EXERCISE:

- ❧ This exercise is an extension; it assumes that you have attained the things you envy. It asks you . . . then what?
- ❧ Fill in the blanks:

  If I got all of this _____, then I would feel _____.

  All this _____ would create in me a sense of _____, and I would be a more _____ person.

- ❧ Question: what are the **qualities** you feel you would attain? These qualities are probably your true soul work, the most basic desires of your soul. Think about how you could acquire these even without all the fill-in-the-blanks.

RETURNING:
Mapping What You Find, Dreaming the Future

LOOKING OVER all the results from the exercises, you now should have quite a collection of attributes and qualities and circumstances to think about. Figuring out how to own them starts with seeing the themes among the disparate people you have written about.

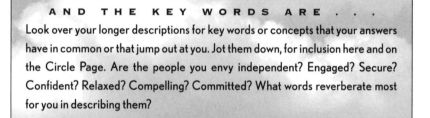

A N D   T H E   K E Y   W O R D S   A R E . . .
Look over your longer descriptions for key words or concepts that your answers have in common or that jump out at you. Jot them down, for inclusion here and on the Circle Page. Are the people you envy independent? Engaged? Secure? Confident? Relaxed? Compelling? Committed? What words reverberate most for you in describing them?

VOCATIONAL CLUES START HERE

AS IN the "Culture that Captures" chapter, your results of the various envy exercises can also hold vocational guidance. If these people are spending their time doing something you envy, have you thought of a variation of that work for yourself?

NINA: "When I do vocational counseling, this is often the most potent section in people's maps. The envy is seldom about lifestyle and trappings, and almost always about a mission and purpose that really appeal to the client."

SOUL MAPPING EXERCISE:

- ❧ Who are the people you envy and what do they do?
- ❧ What are the salient characteristics about them and their work—the specific things about them that you envy?

- ❧ Can you see that you may have gifts in these areas too, even if they are expressed in different ways?
- ❧ How might you go about researching ways to express those gifts or learn more about the areas represented by the people you have named?

CHOOSING YOUR ENVY PRIORITIES FOR THE FUTURE

WHETHER IT'S acting "as if" in order to try embodying a quality, researching a new field to work in, or otherwise claiming attributes first spotted in others, look over your exercises and make a list of priorities. What's most important—a theme that came up? A specific? Both?

SOUL MAPPING EXERCISE:

- ❧ Create a very personal "to do" list of action items that emerged from this chapter. Again, envy work isn't about imitation, but about expressing something in your own way.
- ❧ As you work on the "to do" list, watch for objections, the "yes, buts . . ." Realize that there are many ways envy keeps us safe. If we can just resent the other person, we don't have to risk. There's a cost to the soul of not doing envy work, to be sure. There's also a cost to venturing out with your findings. If you feel stuck in places on your list, do a little cost/promise analysis: the cost of envying and not embodying . . . and the promise that may await you if you do.

BRINGING PRAYER INTO THE PICTURE

IN A chapter so much about tapping envy as a tool for change, we want to be sure to balance all that suggested movement with something more contemplative.

In addition to coming up with personal insights, and acting "as if" to translate the qualities we envy into our own lives, there are also spiritual tools we can use to ask that these qualities somehow come to fruition in our lives. It doesn't mean they will or even should come to fruition. But envy work isn't just ours to bear; we can summon the power of prayer.

Many of us are taught in childhood to pray in general, vague ways—often, to pray only for God's will. But it is also possible to pray for the qualities that you feel you need in your life, and many of these can be the qualities that have come up in your envy scan:

- Praying for serenity.
- Praying for freedom.
- Praying for the creative insights that you need to translate these qualities into your life and make them a reality.

Sometimes, envy is about accepting what we cannot change. Prayer can help here, too. The serenity prayer in Alcoholics Anonymous is a wonderful expression of this: "God grant me the serenity to accept the things I cannot change, the courage to change the things I can, and the wisdom to know the difference."

Sometimes, we need to place God in the empty places in our lives. We may never be millionaires, we may never be in perfect health, we will not live forever. But we can put God in those "empty" places and have a sense of peace and serenity—and acceptance and love for who we already are.

A CONCLUDING PARADOX

SO WE end "envy" with a paradox: to blend desired change with serenity and self-acceptance. To listen to what the soul is saying to you in this chapter, to map it, *and* to not cling to it. We are asking you to appropriate the qualities that you envy, translate them into your life, and make them a part of who you are—while paradoxically accepting at the same time who you are right now, with love and nurture, knowing that God loves you simply the way you are.

The spiritual reality here is one of both growth and peace . . . movement and self-acceptance . . . dynamic insight and peaceful serenity. So when contradictions come up on your Circle Page, don't worry; it's all part of the Soul Mapping process, particularly around the topic of envy. Like our map, we are containers meant to hold contradictions, meant to ultimately grasp the elusive but real blessing amidst our many feelings and paradoxes.

CIRCLE PAGE QUESTIONS

— ✿ —

YOUR CIRCLE PAGE:
What "Angels Are Knocking?"

LOOK OVER all you have written for this chapter. Think of it as a particular journey unto itself, into very specific territory. You return from this exploration with many thoughts and impressions. As a way to start that honing and honoring process, answer these questions quickly and intuitively. You can write directly in your circle or answer the questions on another piece of paper and then transfer the results to the Circle Page. Either way, this is a place to record the most insistent (and possibly most important) data from your responses; a place to capture the "angels knocking" at your door.

- List the qualities and patterns you have come up with in your envy inventories.
- Using crayons or colored pencils, draw some symbols or images that capture these traits.
- Do a little "translating" of your envy desires into possible real life steps. List new steps you can take in the direction of your dream.
- List your associations with the words "serenity" and "peace." Create some symbols that represent these.

SACRED PLACE

OF ALL the answers to exercises in this chapter, which one(s) feel most sacred and important to you at this time in your life?

EMOTION

IS THERE a predominant emotion in your responses to the exercises?

SURPRISE

WHAT MOST surprised you about your responses in this chapter? What do you know now that you did not know before?

NURTURE AND RENEWAL

WHICH ANSWERS spoke the most to a hunger or a longing? Is there an aspect of your answers that, if it were more integrated in your life right now, would be particularly nurturing and helpful to you?

PERSONAL IMPERATIVE

AS YOU review your answers to this chapter, do you sense any imperative arising from what you wrote—any need to change your life? If so, where is the urge for change most insistent in this chapter?

8

SHOULDS, SHOULDN'TS, DON'TS, AND CAN'TS
SELF-LIMITING BELIEFS

————— ❧ —————

"A disciple once came to Abba Joseph, saying, 'Father, according as I

am able, I keep my little rule, my little fast, and my little prayer. And

according as I am able, I strive to cleanse my mind of all evil thoughts

and my heart of all evil intents. Now, what more should I do?'

"Abba Joseph rose up and stretched out his hands to heaven, and

his fingers became like ten lamps of fire. He answered, 'Why not be

totally changed into fire?'"

—Richard Foster, *Prayer*

GETTING THE LAY OF THE LAND

THE ENVY chapter encouraged you to explore a feeling "nice" people supposedly shouldn't have, but in fact everyone does. This chapter continues that exploration, gently, but in a slightly different direction.

While envy comes in many guises, the appearance of envy is usually recognizable as such, and the source of the envy is also identifiable—a person, a lifestyle, a career, etc. The soul also speaks to us through—or is constrained by—subtle rules whose source often isn't obvious. For Soul Mapping purposes, we call these rules our "shoulds," "shouldn'ts," "don'ts" and "can'ts." Since they operate on a conscious and unconscious level, they can have a profound impact on whatever personal or professional change we are trying to achieve through the Soul Mapping process.

We all have internal prohibitions—sometimes they shift with age, and some remain from childhood. They can be quiet or noisy in terms of how they direct us. Guilt, or the threat of it, is often their companion. A shouldn't is much more subtle than "don't murder." A shouldn't is often about desires or longings so hidden they are more like quiet impossibilities. Their sources are many: they derive from the rules about behavior and life that we have gotten from the culture, our parents, our friends, our work environment. In this way, they are different from the desires and yearnings in the following chapter. Those "faint calls" originate someplace deep within *you*; this chapter is after the rules that have a more external source.

The shoulds, shouldn'ts, don'ts and can'ts may be subtle and hard to detect, but their effects are not: they show up in passivity, self-sabotage, and other ways we have of undermining ourselves. In many of the Soul Mapping chapters, we ask you to "hold the tension" between what comes up on your maps vis à vis the future and where you are now; out of this creative tension your future is trying to emerge. That future may never get a chance if the shoulds and shouldn'ts are not clarified.

If one of the Soul Mapping goals is to help you live out your true potential, you may have to go beyond your own inner prohibitions and limiting values about yourself. The purpose of this chapter is to unpack some of your beliefs about yourself and identify areas where your shoulds and shouldn'ts have proven life-limiting.

BEGINNING EXPLORATIONS:
Surveying the Past and the Present

TRAVELING THROUGH the terrain of our various prohibitions means a first stop in childhood. All of us probably heard admonitions like these when we were growing up:

Don't cross the street without a grownup.

Watch your step.

You shouldn't slouch.

Don't speak with food in your mouth.

Hold your pencil that way.

Sit up straight.

Stop making that funny face, or your face will get stuck and never go back to its natural expression.

This short list represents but a tiny fraction of the prohibitions, beliefs and values communicated to us via our family and community. Some shoulds and shouldn'ts are meant to protect us from danger. After all, kids shouldn't play with matches, knives or razor blades. But other shoulds are simply the values our parents held and which they wanted us to hold, too.

Different families have very different beliefs about how dangerous the world is, what constitutes acceptable social behavior, and how you express family loyalty as you grow up. We internalize a surprising number of these shoulds and shouldn'ts. We incorporate them into our personal belief system and operate as if they are true and normal life assumptions.

QUICK FLASH FROM THE PAST

What are the first shoulds and shouldn'ts that surface for you as you think back to your childhood? The truisms told to you; the things that were supposed to keep you safe and the world in order? One woman doing this exercise immediately remembered "GM": "Good manners." That was paramount in her family. What are the key words you associate with this chapter title? The rest of the exercises will take you deeper with the results.

BACK TO THE SOURCE THAT IS FAMILY

WE ALL had a mother and father, and probably siblings. We observed those people in our family and they continually influenced us. What we heard and saw as children—the attitudes, the conflicts, what was left unsaid and undone in our families—combined to shape our adult beliefs about reality. These basic beliefs still operate powerfully in our adult lives, whether consciously or unconsciously.

Such beliefs start in the repetitive patterns that we as children observed in our families—in the behavior of our parents, aunts and uncles, and all the other players in our family drama. What we saw and lived as children becomes, in a very real way, the expectational set for what we call *normal* in our adult lives. Often, we don't realize we hold such beliefs until we run into a way of relating to the world that reflects a contrary, conflicting view. We may then make a judgment that the person who holds such an alien view is not "normal." We may find the other person unappealing, boring, or simply inconsistent with our expectations about what is right.

Jean Piaget, the Swiss cognitive psychologist, coined the term egocentrism as a way of describing a young child's tendency to view reality only from his or her perspective. KEN offers an illustration:

"When my daughter Kirsten was three, she wanted to show me a lovely picture she had drawn. But she didn't turn it toward me when I asked to see it. She simply assumed that I could see it from her perspective. Such young children feel that their own perspective is the only possible truth, but as they grow, they "de-center" and become able to view reality from a variety of other vantage points."

Yet some of us remain psychologically egocentric, continuing to view and judge the world from our family experience alone. This self-centered tendency then limits our judgment and choices.

WHEN SOMEONE ELSE'S "SHOULD" IS YOUR "STRANGE"

EGOCENTRISM OFTEN appears in shoulds and shouldn'ts. Often we don't see them clearly until we have exposure to another family system, and even then they may show up as the other person's strangeness, not as clarity about what we grew up with! Marriage or intimate relationships often challenge our definitions of "normal."

Consider the story of John and Lisa. John grew up in a large Irish-Catholic family that he describes as "quiet and peaceful, with very little conflict." People would work out their differences, call a family meeting, or pout quietly until conflicts blew over. John grew up and married Lisa, who came from an Italian family that she described as "volatile." There were regular weekend fights between her parents and among her siblings. People fought openly with great emotional volume. Yet her family was also very affectionate and physical with one another.

These two very different family styles collided in John and Lisa's marriage. Lisa would get angry and shout over some issue, and John would retreat into silence, thinking that the marriage was over or that Lisa was crazy. John's family background gave him no category for Lisa's behavior. Likewise, Lisa couldn't deal with John's pouting and silence. She wondered why he didn't talk. She experienced his silence as annoying. Both parties assumed that their own style was normal, and the other's was not.

It takes hard work to overcome such hidden loyalties and styles and realize that another person is simply different from the way we are. Making that adjustment means letting go of our need to change others. It means accepting them and loving them for the very qualities that so challenge us.

We can begin to see that our beliefs profoundly affect the way we perceive the world and the way we behave in it. We also see, as John and Lisa did, that most of us tend to question or even reject life opportunities for which we have no basic category in our prior experience. If you had no category for financial success in your family of origin, for instance, you might well feel uneasy or ambivalent about financial success in your adult life.

In speaking about the privation of her childhood, the noted poet and author Maya Angelou stated "I had to reinvent myself as an adult." Having a limited repertoire of categories means we must "reinvent ourselves" if we are to reach our potential and live a full and relatively free life. It also means we may have to free ourselves from the shoulds and shouldn'ts that we learned growing up.

SOUL MAPPING EXERCISE:

❧ Assuming a certain amount of egocentrism was operating in your family, jot down some of rules about what was "normal" behavior and what was not. The term egocentrism does not imply judgment here; it's merely descriptive: What were the **prevailing perspectives** as you were growing up? Was it "normal" to be quiet? Opinionated? Cheerful? Resentful? Cautious?

❧ Alternatively, what was definitely not "normal" and stood out and got commented on when you saw it in other families?

SURFACING YOUR FAMILIAL SHOULDS AND SHOULDN'TS

HOW DO you continue to identify what you learned in childhood? One place to consult is the results of the exercises in the "Childhood" chapter of this book. Some key words may indicate the shoulds, shouldn'ts and can'ts that prevailed and may still prevail for you. Another way is to do a narrative of your family history, focusing on both sides of the family, and what they brought to the mix.

KEN shows how the narrative works, by using his own family as an example:

"I grew up in Minnesota, where, in the words of Garrison Keillor, 'All the women are strong, all the men are good looking, and all the children are above average.'

"My mother was one of nine children born to a Norwegian immigrant couple. As a child, she lived on the plains of western Minnesota in a house without indoor plumbing. My mother was a large woman, "big-boned" she used to say. She was very capable, hard-working, and self-assured to the point of self-righteousness. During the first eight years of my childhood, she occupied herself as an able housewife and mother. Then, when I was eight years old, she and my father purchased a variety store in a small city. We all managed the store together. My mother was the bookkeeper, sales clerk, and inventory manager. She proved herself to be a cooperative and effective partner to my father.

"Even though the story has hardly begun, you can already begin to see the outlines and the quality of the categories I internalized as the son of this particular woman, my mother.

Women are strong and capable.

Women are loyal and supportive of men.

Women are able to work as entrepreneurs and effective managers.

Also, women are "big." That is, they are able to make things right. They nurture, hold, move mountains.

"Yet my mother also had a shadow side to her. She had a certain contempt for my father, who was quite emotionally expressive, particularly with his anger. She felt that people should rein in their feelings and not complain about discomfort.

She considered people who expressed their emotions to be weak, pathetic and unmanly. My mother could be particularly critical of my father, children and neighbors. She reserved special criticism for women who set a bad example by smoking. She called smoking cigarettes 'a filthy habit.' Men were somehow exempt from this charge. She was also highly critical of disorder. She categorized a disheveled bedroom as a 'shameful mess.' Yet she lacked the relational tools to get family members to change their patterns. Therefore, she was the one to clean up the 'shameful messes,' which would further fuel her criticism. Growing up with my mother meant that people in our family learned to believe they could criticize each other, but could not complain about their own life conditions.

"My father was the only child of an ethnically German family. For much of his childhood, his father was absent and his mother and grandmother were very indulgent with him. Then, through his young adult life during the depression, he endured a degree of poverty and had to nurse both his ill mother and invalid grandmother.

"He was an emotional man who, within our family, expressed his feelings vigorously. Everyone knew when Dad was 'mad' or frustrated. My father was also a controlled alcoholic throughout my childhood, and some of his emotional outbursts were fueled by alcohol.

"My father took a series of sales jobs while I was growing up and proved to be an excellent salesman. To explain his success, he would say that he could 'feel people's pain,' another way of saying that he was highly empathic and could anticipate customers' needs and questions.

"He was a hard worker who believed in 'saving for a rainy day.' Thrifty to the point of being cheap, he was a strong believer in deferred gratification. For example, my parents often talked about going to Hawaii together someday, but the plan was constantly put off. In fact, they never did go to Hawaii. What had been a dream became a regret when my mother died unexpectedly in 1970."

PSYCHOLOGICAL ARCHEOLOGY:
LESSONS LEARNED IN THE FAMILY SYSTEM

GIVEN THE plots and subplots in KEN's descriptive vignette, what beliefs about life, men, women, work, money, etc., did he grow up with? What were his shoulds and shouldn'ts? What were the dos and don'ts? What were the rules? Here's an incomplete list he came up with:

Adults should work very hard.

People should save money and limit their expenses.

Husbands and wives can work together.

It's a good thing to go into business for yourself.

Enjoying your life should not be a central priority.

Men are frustrated, emotional individuals.

A good woman is self-sufficient, supportive, and contemptuous of men.

Good women are the emotional and domestic custodians of the family.

You should be loyal to your marriage and stay in it at all costs.

You can begin to see how this particular psychological archaeology works. As we examine our operative family value systems, we unearth powerful messages and beliefs about the way life should operate—beliefs that may be counter to how our emerging *soul* wants life to operate.

SOUL MAPPING EXERCISE:
PSYCHOLOGICAL ARCHAEOLOGY AROUND BELIEFS

- Write down the names of your significant family members—parents, siblings, grandparents, uncles, aunts, etc.
- What beliefs about life, men, women, work, money, etc., did each family member convey to you? Look over KEN's list for ways you can phrase these results.
- What were some of the taboos that your parents upheld?
- What were some of the expectations they had for what you should or should not do with your life?

FORMATION BY DISAPPOINTMENT

IN ADDITION to the attitudes and stances taken by your parents, you also need to consider the fateful consequences they experienced as a normal part of living. We tend to internalize reality, particularly the harsh aspects, as a normal part of adult existence. For KEN, the fateful consequences imbued in his growing up were around the family business.

"Our variety store nearly failed several times, despite my parents' hard work. Over ten years, two major fires in an adjoining grocery cut our customer base radically. Then a major shopping mall opened two miles away and drew away nearly all our customers.

"The fateful message in these events—which I heard from my father's slips of the tongue—was: 'You work hard only to be rewarded with failure.' Work is not met with success. Efforts do not bear fruit. Indeed, effort is punished. My father finally moved to a small town, purchased a small variety store which he knew would be his last, and eventually retired. His life bore out the premise that dreams don't become realities; that fate conspires against people, no matter how hard they work. This thesis was borne out again in my mother's untimely illness and eventual death."

A child observing unfolding events can easily internalize the tragic dimension of a family history as an unconscious expectational set. This is how life happens.

Despite a conscious determination *not* to repeat or re-enact one's parents' fate, the forces of expectation do work powerfully. In adult life, the child may have a subtle, yet inexorable, tendency to reenact the parents' fate, thought patterns, and operative "should" system.

SOUL MAPPING EXERCISE:

- &9 Are there any negative expectations associated with the shoulds and shouldn'ts that you have uncovered so far?
- &9 Were any of your family's beliefs weighted toward adverse outcomes or expected disappointment?

WHEN ALTERNATE POSSIBILITIES APPEAR

OFTEN, OTHER family members appear on the scene to temper the parental messages we get. These sources of alternate beliefs can be grandparents, an important aunt or uncle, older siblings—even neighbors or other community figures. KEN had two such figures:

"My paternal grandfather lived with us during most of my childhood. Patient and self-possessed, he spent a great deal of time reading to his grandchildren and instilling in them certain values, particularly thrift and the importance of regular practice of anything in which we wished to excel. Lacking even a high school education, he was self-taught and self-disciplined. He was constantly working to improve his penmanship and vocabulary.

"Here was an alternative set of beliefs! Through my grandfather, I learned you could improve yourself with effort, and there was a world of books and knowledge that could empower you, if you put in the effort.

"Uncle Jack was another important figure, an unlikely character in such a Midwestern drama. Born in Spain and an immigrant from Cuba, Uncle Jack was a chef at the Drake Hotel in Chicago and an avid cigar-smoker. He would come to our home in Minnesota and cook gourmet meals that we wouldn't eat. Jack would throw a fit, sometimes flinging the food in frustration. I recall braised celery flying through the dining room and hitting the wall. He was quick-tempered, but quick to apologize. He spoke with a Spanish accent and rolled his own Havana cigars. He told stories about Cuba and what it was like to live in Chicago.

"This character, who was a regular fixture in our home on holidays, was a refreshing and invigorating influence. He communicated his message not so much in details, but in his presence. He was living evidence of a wider world beyond our own: a great city called Chicago, foreign countries, accents, different cultures and ways of thinking.

"Having a person in the family who left his country of origin and became successful in a big city provided my sister and me with new possibilities. Uncle Jack offered us new categories for our imaginings. And as I say, you can only do what you can imagine."

SOUL MAPPING EXERCISE:

- What people did you come in contact with in your childhood or adolescence who tempered the parental shoulds and shouldn'ts that prevailed?
- List the alternate beliefs that these people communicated to you.
- Were any of those beliefs important in your own formation?
- Are there any you need to re-visit, or draw on now?

TRAVELING DEEPER:
Charting New Territory

CHECK YOUR MULTIPLE SOURCES OF SHOULDN'TS

WHILE THE "Beginning Explorations" section concentrated on the family as the source of many of our formative beliefs, as we grow older other environments join our family system as powerful influences on our shoulds and shouldn'ts.

These environments include the culture we live in, the work environment we spend our days in, as well as the gender expectations sea we all swim in, which we discuss later. Not everything in your environment represents a block or a goad in the wrong direction for you. Some rules of your environment simply won't matter to you. But it's important to float them up, to be aware of what you're swimming in, so that you can determine what is helpful guidance and what subtly underminines you.

SOUL MAPPING EXERCISE: THE "RULES SCAN":
TABOOS, SUBTLE AND OTHERWISE

- Do a scan of the rules that prevailed during your life so far. This is similar to the "envy scan" exercise in Chapter 7, except it asks you to look at what was forbidden—or simply frowned upon—at various stages of your past. (**Note**: Of course we're not talking about things that are clearly against the law, like various crimes. This is a place to track the various constraints at work at different times and in different environments, as well as what was forbidden.)

∂ Review the following periods of your life. For each period, also list the environments you were subject to: home, school, work, other.

> Childhood, birth to age 10.
> Adolescence, ages 10-18.
> Young adulthood, ages 18-30.
> Your life after age 30.

∂ For each period, what were the shoulds and shouldn'ts? What were the dos and don'ts? Realize that shoulds and shouldn'ts are often flip sides of each other. For example, you "should be successful" and you "shouldn't work at a job that pays little" are essentially about the same thing, but with different emphases.

∂ What were the overall rules that prevailed in these environments?

∂ What hopes and goals were implicit in those rules?

∂ How did you react at the time to the prohibitions or urgings that were in the air?

∂ Are any of them still at work in your life?

EARLY FAILURE: WHERE THE "CAN'TS" CAN COME FROM

IN ADDITION to our family values and beliefs, we also run into personal failures and disappointments as adolescents and young adults. Often these disappointments lead to a premature conclusion that we "can't" do this or that activity. Or we may conclude that we have no ability in a certain field.

KEN remembers receiving a clarinet for his eleventh birthday. "I was both pleased and surprised by the chance to play a musical instrument. However, after three months of lessons from an impatient teacher and weeks of agonizing practice without family help, (no one in my family could read notes or play an instrument), I gave up the clarinet. I simply was never able to master sightreading, rhythm, fingering, and all the other concurrent skills needed to play.

"I concluded from this painful experience that I was 'bad' at music. Although I continued to listen to music, I shrank away from any real involvement in it or any kind of music-making. Eleven years later, after taking some piano lessons with a wonderfully patient college professor, I realized that my earlier clarinet experience was simply an unfortunate combination of having the wrong teacher and not being ready to play.

"My mother never ice-skated after she fell and banged her head on the ice at the age of twelve. I remember her unwillingness to go on the ice when the rest of the family was skating. For my mother, ice-skating became a chosen disability."

How many of us "write off" whole areas of human experience after such a bad experience in adolescence? Every time we make such choices, our lives become a little narrower. The whole Soul Mapping process is about getting to wider spaces, and seeing ourselves as bigger than we think we are. To get to those open spaces in adulthood, we need to identify the places where the can'ts keep us shrunk.

SOUL MAPPING EXERCISE:

- ❧ What failures, struggles, or disappointments did you experience as an adolescent or young adult?
- ❧ What conclusions can you draw from these difficult experiences? Have you distanced yourself from the areas of life they represent?
- ❧ How can you recover from these disappointments? Can you learn from the experiences in any way?
- ❧ Come up with some activities you can undertake that would be healing and restorative with regard to these early experiences. From his clarinet disaster, for example, KEN chose to buy a Congo drum and learn more about percussion.

BEWARE SUBTLE GUISES:
PERFECTIONISM AND THE "WHATEVER" PATTERN

OUR RESPONSES to the conscious and unconscious shoulds and shouldn'ts in our lives can manifest in two extremes, neither of which helps us live out our true potential.

One approach is to *embrace* various shoulds in such a way that we become perfectionistic. It is one thing to have high standards, but quite another to be overly demanding of yourself in every area of life, from eating habits to work achievement to a keeping perfectly tidy house. People with an overly perfectionistic pattern of judgment seem to have internalized a stern parental voice that has high expectations and threatens punitive consequences for failure. We remember a client berating herself for forgetting her checkbook, calling herself "stupid and irresponsible."

Clearly, such a perfectionistic value belief system lacks a sense of mercy or forgiveness. Everything is a "big deal." Ironically, several studies of perfectionistic people show that they tend to be underachievers, or that they take excessive time to accomplish tasks. They procrastinate out of fear of not getting things perfectly right, so their very perfectionism tends to expand the time necessary to finish a task.

Consider our friend Todd, who almost called off his wedding because of all the challenging tasks that accompanied the process of planning a wedding, setting up a home, supporting his future family, and so on. In his mind, all these tasks had to be completed perfectly.

If you have such a perfectionist style, it's important to find ways of noticing the pattern, naming it and modifying it so that it becomes a more reasonable, forgiving style. Introducing a sense of humor can be a wonderful antidote. You might also consider getting some counseling if your patterns of perfectionism really limit your life.

If perfectionism takes inner shoulds and prohibitions too seriously, the "whatever" pattern takes the opposite approach, and is just as limiting. This pattern is about appearing not to care one way or another about anything. It may be a way of avoiding one's shoulds and shouldn'ts; it's also a way of avoiding engagement, commitment and life's possible failures and disappointments.

If nothing really matters anyway, it's impossible to be hurt. This is a protective, cynical stance, with the term "whatever" its motto. This refusal to engage sincerely in a value system, or claim goals for oneself, results in a phlegmatic, sullen lifestyle with few highs or lows.

Since nothing really matters, the practitioner of the "whatever" pattern gets neither excited nor disappointed about life. Likewise, he or she doesn't get particularly worked up about events, whether good or bad ones.

If this is your style, try to recognize that it's probably a fear-based defense. Underneath the pattern, you will discern a hidden set of desires, hopes, and goals. If you can begin to admit this to yourself and gradually claim what you want, you can move up and out of this paralyzing pattern. Realize also that when the soul speaks, it may be softly, but it's *not* in the language of "whatever." Our deepest desires have an insistent quality about them that is the opposite of the sigh or mutter of whatever.

SOUL MAPPING EXERCISE:

- ❧ Check yourself for perfectionism or the "whatever" pattern: Do either sound familiar to you?
- ❧ Do you tend to be perfectionistic? Where does that tendency come from?
- ❧ Do you identify with the "whatever" pattern? If so, what areas of life are you truly passionate about? Name them and find ways of expressing this sincere interest and passion—through actions, in speaking to others, etc.

RETURNING:
Mapping What You Find, Dreaming the Future

USE A PLACE OF CURRENT TENSION

DOING THE exercises in this chapter means you emerge with an array of information about the subtle formative beliefs in your life and how they manifest as shoulds, shouldn'ts, don'ts and can'ts.

But this chapter is not just about the rules themselves: Shoulds and shouldn'ts are about the place where the beliefs and rules, subtle or otherwise, butt up against our individual hopes and become decisions or patterns that involve discounting what we really want.

For this "returning" part of the journey, we encourage you to emerge with something you can work on now—a current example of where past prohibitions impede the future in some way. To find an example, look for a place of current tension in your life.

For example a client named Mary has a strong desire to take a sabbatical—to truly do nothing for six months to a year. She claims to not really have known this, but it was the first thing to pop up as she did her map. The shouldn'ts she hears that are opposed to any sabbatical are about responsibility, money, thriftiness, and work habits. These prohibitions, with their various sources, have so far thwarted the sabbatical, but not the longing. That longing is persistent enough to sound like a true cry of the soul, a cry for something that goes far beyond logistics, finances, or the need to explain a gap on a resume to someone. Whatever Mary decides to do, she needs to *engage* both the longing and the prohibition. Something new may be trying to emerge in her life.

Soul Mapping is about embracing the repudiated parts of the self and bringing these aspects back into active consciousness. Shoulds and shouldn'ts and can'ts are often the means by which our deep longings are repudiated and are made to seem "bad." It's important to dust off the layer of judgment that lies on these longings, see whose judgment it is, and determine where you want to go from here.

SOUL MAPPING EXERCISE:

- ৪৹ Think of a current example of a shouldn't tension from your life now. If you're having trouble, use guilt as a locator; guilt is the emotion that often accompanies the thought of doing something that goes up against a prohibition.
- ৪৹ What is the tension about? What are the two sides, i.e., what you want to do and the should or shouldn't it gets tangled up with?
- ৪৹ How valid is the should or shouldn't? Where does it come from?
- ৪৹ Do you see any way for what you want to do and the prohibition to be reconciled with each other? Do they share any common ground? This question is not as strange as it sounds. In the example of Mary's sabbatical, the prohibition stemmed from rules about being a **good steward** of financial resources and not doing anything financially risky. But her longing for rest and renewal **also** sprang from the desire to be a good steward—of her health, time, and soul. When Mary saw that these two opposing views had such an important root in common, she began to think of ways to craft a financially viable sabbatical.

What's underneath?

SOUL WORK often involves a descent, and this chapter is no exception. Go back to the results of your rule scan, or the exercise above, or any exercise in this chapter, and think about what may be underneath the prohibitions.

Some rules (though not all) have roots in beliefs that are unstated. For example: "You shouldn't leave that well-paying job just because you don't like it" can stem from a larger belief, like: "Work isn't supposed to be enjoyable." Or: "If you leave this chance to make money, you may not get another."

Beneath even *those* beliefs lies basic, primal stuff: fear . . . a scarcity mentality . . . fatalism . . . a belief you don't deserve to be happy . . . a worry about competence . . . a dislike for risk. These warnings are not bad per se; indeed, it's good to hear and possibly to heed their message. The problem is when you do not identify the subliminal prohibition, and it manifests itself not in a conscious way, but in a thwarting of your desires.

SOUL MAPPING EXERCISE:

- ❧ Select a should or a shouldn't from the previous exercise, or take a few ones from your family of origin.
- ❧ Close your eyes, take a deep breath, and repeat the should or shouldn't to yourself, silently or aloud. Write it down in big letters at the top of a page. Look at it; let it look back at you. Ask yourself: What are the underpinnings of this rule? What beliefs are the bedrock it rests on?
- ❧ What is the source of these beliefs? You, your family, the culture?
- ❧ Try this exercise again with some additional shoulds and shouldn'ts. See whether you get some similar themes among the beliefs that emerge.

WEIGHING WHAT YOU FIND

LOOK AT the beliefs that emerged for you in this exercise, especially ones from your past—the beliefs that supported the shoulds and shouldn'ts from your childhood. Pick the most powerful, prevalent ones. Are these beliefs operating in your life today? If so, how do they show up? Are they disguised, or remarkably similar to the beliefs you ran into in the past?

SOUL MAPPING EXERCISE:

- ❧ Look at your most powerful and prevalent past beliefs and how they show up in your life now.
- ❧ To borrow the key question from short-term cognitive therapy—Are these beliefs in your best interest? If so, why? If not, what can you do to lessen their influence in your life?

YOUR CURRENT DEFINITION OF FREEDOM

ALL TOO often, the shoulds, shouldn'ts, don'ts, and can'ts are the things that huddle, supposedly in our corner and on our side, and whose job it is to keep us safe. To locate the most prevalent prohibition in your life now—and perhaps to locate the thing you most need on a soul level—ask yourself:

How would I define *freedom* at this point in my life now?

This freedom is not about stepping on someone else, but perhaps it *is* about stepping out in some way. Are you leaving anyone behind in the stepping out? Moving beyond the people in your life in any way is threatening to all concerned. Let this threat identify itself if it needs to.

This freedom is about awareness of the self-limiting beliefs and prohibitions that can all too easily assume an autopilot function in our lives. Take what you wrote for your freedom and listen to it for the wisdom and guidance it holds.

THE SOULFUL WORK OF IMAGINING

AS KEN likes to point out in his work with clients, you can do only what you can imagine. As an process, Soul Mapping asks you to *imagine* a world beyond the self-limiting beliefs we all grew up with. Imagining that world does not mean trying to discredit the beliefs, or dismissing them; then they just pop up in even more disguised and unhelpful ways.

Imagining a different world *does* mean bringing the beliefs to consciousness; recognizing them for what they are—thoughts, not facts; and moving on, to offer the world and yourself a new set of words to live by. Let this chapter be a place to acknowledge the past rules . . . *and* authorize the new ones, even the ones that, in the words of the opening quote, totally change you into fire.

Circle Page Questions

—— ❧ ——

Your Circle Page:
What "Angels Are Knocking?"

LOOK OVER all you have written for this chapter. Think of it as a particular journey unto itself, into very specific territory. You return from this exploration with many thoughts and impressions. As a way to start that honing and honoring process, answer these questions quickly and intuitively. You can write directly in your circle or answer the questions on another piece of paper and then transfer the results to the Circle Page. Either way, this is a place to record the most insistent (and possibly most important) data from your responses; a place to capture the "angels knocking" at your door.

- List some of the family beliefs from your past which have been limiting. These may have to do with gender, your family birth order, your reputation in the family, familial expectations of you or other influences.
- Fill in the blanks in this sentence: _____ (your name) could never do _____ because he/she is just too _____. You may want to do this exercise several times.
- List a few of your life disappointments and failures. Find images or symbols that represent these experiences.
- Name one or two secret passions or desires that seem so forbidden or impractical or inadmissible that they would be embarrassing to share. Use symbols to show these.

SACRED PLACE

OF ALL the answers to exercises in this chapter, which one(s) feel most sacred and important to you at this time in your life?

EMOTION

IS THERE a predominant emotion in your responses to the exercises?

SURPRISE

WHAT MOST surprised you about your responses in this chapter? What do you know now that you did not know before?

NURTURE AND RENEWAL

WHICH ANSWERS spoke the most to a hunger or a longing? Is there an aspect of your answers that, if it were more integrated in your life right now, would be particularly nurturing and helpful to you?

PERSONAL IMPERATIVE

AS YOU review your answers to this chapter, do you sense any imperative arising from what you wrote—any need to change your life? If so, where is the urge for change most insistent in this chapter?

FAINT CALLS AND SMALL VOICES
Hidden Desires, Dreams, and Yearnings

"For over the margins of life comes a whisper, a faint call,

a premonition of richer living which we know we are passing by."

–Quaker author Thomas R. Kelly, *A Testament of Devotion*

Getting the Lay of the Land

THE WORK of clarifying, acknowledging and moving beyond our internal prohibitions is the work of the prior chapter. "Faint Calls and Small Voices," on the other hand, asks you to look at the flip side of internal prohibitions—to shift from looking at what you feel you should or shouldn't do to what your soul *wants* to do on a deep level.

This chapter is about paying heed to faint signs, glimmers, surprises, experiences and coincidences that come to us "out of left field." These faint callings could come in a dream, a sudden experience of beauty, a spiritual epiphany, or they could arrive through the inadvertent comment of a friend. Faint calls can also be the small, insistent voices tugging at us—the little events we dismiss as silly or impractical, or the childhood dreams we have long put away. This is a chapter about resurrecting and attending to those little voices, urgings, and old dreams we have long put to bed.

The emphasis here is different than in Chapter Four, which is about pleasures and pastimes. That chapter is for yearnings that are so strong they are already manifest in things you actually do or imagine doing; this chapter will try to tease the fainter signals out of you—the dreams and desires that lie just beneath the surface. They often stay there, buried, because they seem impractical, or impossible, or simply too faint. But if brought to the surface and literally given space on your Soul Map, these yearnings often clearly link up with talents and hoped-for directions in life that perhaps you never articulated before.

Because this chapter is not so much about immediate reality as about things harbored and kept to yourself, it will encourage you to free associate, to search for clues and energy in the impractical and the supposedly unlikely. This chapter will also traffic in topics we don't talk about too freely: secret lives, sexual fantasies, dreams, reveries, symbols, synchronicities, etc. This is mysterious stuff, and we will not be trying to pin down what everything *means*. We will be asking you to pay attention, to be playful, to tease out direction from these ongoing sources of energy and insight.

A SOULFUL INTEGRITY

THE GOAL of this chapter's process is not necessarily to change a career path or make a major life shift. Listening to our "faint callings" can help our lives grow, making them bigger and fuller. Eric Erikson, in his book *On the Seven Stages of Man*, writes about the stage of later life he calls "Integrity vs. Despair." According to Erikson, the healthy human being has lived life with such inner integrity that he or she can look back at life with virtually no regret. Erickson defines inner integrity as that inner impulse in us which honors all of our potential and longings. Paying attention to the promptings of our unconscious mind and the subtle calls of reality can aid us in living out that fullness without regret.

Our relentless, goal-driven approach toward living can cause us to miss engaging these subtle aspects of experience. Like workhorses wearing blinders, we plunge onward to the next task we think is important, never seeing what is coming to us from the left or right, or above. While it is important to have goals and make an effort towards them, it is also important to develop *peripheral vision* and awareness of the unexpected as it comes to us. The goal in this chapter is not so much to be focused as to be *awake* to meanings and possibilities. In this way, this chapter is a microcosm of the entire Soul Mapping process.

BEGINNING EXPLORATIONS:
Surveying the Past and the Present

AS WITH many of the Soul Mapping explorations, we want to start first in the rich territory of childhood, and track how the desires, dreams, and yearnings of this time may still speak to you today.

CHILDHOOD DREAMS

A LIFE you may long for now may well include old childhood dreams that you have left behind. We need you to dust these off for your Soul Map. Giving them voice can give you a valuable glimpse into what excites and motivates you. There is a certain purity to childhood dreams. They are unsullied by the disappointments and prohibitions of adult reality.

SOUL MAPPING EXERCISE: EXAMINE YOUR CHILDHOOD DREAMS

- What did you want to be when you grew up? List what you can remember. Go back as far is you can. Include your childhood passions on the list: those activities that you couldn't get enough of, that certain game, that hobby, that sport, that interest, that musical instrument.
- Now look over this wonderful list. Carry it around with you for a few days.
- Write a few words next to each item on your list, describing what you liked about it. Look over these qualities. Do you see any patterns or recurring themes that emerge? Write them down in bold crayons, using the appropriate color for each quality that you come up with.
- How do the patterns or recurring themes you found play a role in your life today?

YOUR SECRET LIVES

WE ALL have a secret life—unspoken thoughts and fantasies we harbor. Maybe the secret thoughts and impulses are too shameful or fantastic or out of character for you to share with other people. Nevertheless, they are a window to your true self and true longings, and can therefore be golden nuggets of information that can help you in putting together your Soul Map.

Your secret life is an aspect of your shadow: areas of the self that have been repudiated or hidden from public view. The shadow has come to have "dark" connotations, i.e., it contains all the parts of ourselves that are not nice, or light, or supposedly presentable. The concept of shadow is actually bigger than that. Author and analyst Marie Louise von Franz, who worked with Carl Jung, the originator of the concept of the shadow, pointed out that as we approach our unconscious, the shadow is a name for all that is within us that we cannot directly know. Because it taps into the unconscious, Soul Mapping as a process will bring shadow material to the surface. As that material comes up, we make decisions about whether to "own" it, as it were, or circumscribe it and split it off from our "normal" life. Integrating our shadows—both the seemingly positive and negative things about ourselves that surface—is a lifelong task, and very much a goal of the Soul Mapping process.

SOUL MAPPING EXERCISE: NAMING THE SECRET LIVES

- ❧ Think about what the phrase "your secret life" connotes for you. Use any period of your life: childhood, adolescence, young adulthood, middle age, today's age. Get descriptive: use adjectives, geographic settings, etc.
- ❧ What have you always wanted to do if you could? Suspend all disbelief: What would you do if **anything** were possible?
- ❧ What sort of "secret life" do you think about, or perhaps even engage in? What secret wishes are split off from what you think is possible?
- ❧ During your life so far, what secret wishes got suppressed? What dreams were deferred?

   Note: Depending on your response, there may be a natural tie-in here with the "Envy" chapter, or even some duplication. That's okay. The point is to surface the information, and repetition is worth noting as something the soul really wants to hear.

ESCAPE FANTASIES

Your escape fantasies represent another aspect of your secret life. We occasionally hear clients say "I just want to run away!" Picking up on this remark, we ask: "Where would you run away to? With whom? And what would you do?"

All of us long to "get out" when the going gets tough. Going a little further with this impulse can give you more information for your Soul Map beyond literally running away.

SOUL MAPPING EXERCISE: EXPLORE AN ESCAPE FANTASY

- ◆ If you were to "escape your life" as it is and had the resources to do it, where would you go? Why? And what would you do there? Flesh this out into a paragraph. Be imaginative and inventive in describing your new escape life. Look for pictures in magazines that capture the appeal for you.
- ◆ Now distill some of the *qualities* of this escape life that stand out. List them.
- ◆ Translate some of these qualities into your real life. How could you incorporate them into your life as it really is? Make some suggestions to yourself.

———— ◆ ————

TRAVELING DEEPER:
Charting New Territory

AS WE move deeper into the territory of this chapter, we approach parts of our lives that may be very hidden, indeed. Like more "surface" aspects of our maps, the results of these exercises are important pieces of the puzzle.

EXPLORING YOUR SEXUAL FANTASIES

ONE ASPECT of your secret life is your sexual fantasies. Taking an objective look at them can enable you to see patterns of longing that can be important and illuminating in honestly defining your path. This is a part of your Soul Map you may want to keep confidential, and drafting it may well free you to be more honest and forthright in naming your sexual fantasies.

Here's an example. Jennifer longed for a loving relationship with a man. In counseling, she would talk about her sexual fantasies about this man or that man. When asked to describe these fantasies, she told a detailed story in which she and a particular man were in Paris, walking hand-in-hand along the Seine. The fantasy involved a lot of holding and being together. It was a very warm, romantic fantasy with little explicit sexual action. This was just one of many similar fantasies Jennifer had. In looking at them, it was clear she longed for safety, security and the intimacy of being held.

She also put herself in beautiful settings—Paris, Vienna, Prague. And her imagined companion was always a man who provided a degree of protection and took initiative with her. Clearly, there was a pattern of longing for protection, safety and intimacy. And a wish for beauty and some adventure.

Everyone has some sexual fantasy pattern which comes from unresolved family dynamics that have become sexualized.

Roger is attracted to strong, dominating women. His sexual fantasies often involved him being controlled or dominated by a large, powerful woman. Pleasing a woman is very important to him. Roger's pattern of sexual longing involves getting the security and protective love of a woman and having her approval and praise.

None of this means Roger must marry, or work for, a large, dominating woman! Roger's fantasies simply provide more true information for Roger to build into his Soul Map. There are many other concurrent longings that are equally true for him.

Sexual longings are basic to our unique temperament and makeup, and we ignore or suppress them at our peril. The danger in ignoring them is that they will emerge in a split-off, hidden way that is not integrated with our true self and our everyday life.

SOUL MAPPING EXERCISE: INVITE SEXUAL FANTASIES

ବ Describe four or five sexual fantasies, focusing particularly on recurrent fantasies.

ବ Devote one paragraph to each sexual fantasy, describing the general narrative, plot, characters, etc.

ବ What patterns do you see? And what goals or emotional outcomes do you see in these sexual fantasies?

❧ Translate the patterns you see in your sexual fantasies into qualities you need in your life. Move through any self-shaming impulses you may feel. Let yourself admit your longings. It's not necessary to be practical, realistic or entirely integrated when engaging these fantasies. Let them be a part of your overall Soul Map. Trust that your unconscious can find a way to bring them into your life in a constructive and vibrant way.

LISTENING TO YOUR UNCONSCIOUS

THE WORD "unconscious" conjures images of realms that are mysterious, shrouded, and impossible to discern clearly. Yet is the unconscious mind really such a stranger to us? Not at all. We live alongside it everyday. We see it in our dreams. When we daydream, the unconscious reveals itself in the fantasies and reveries that course through our minds. We glimpse it in certain objects that holds special significance for us—perhaps in photographs of certain cherished people, personal objects, or even works of art that we encounter. All these familiar pieces somehow fit into the larger mosaic.

We might not be able to see the whole picture in clear focus on any given day, yet with the right awareness and practice, we can glimpse the unconscious and use it to build new and useful bridges to our true self.

Often, we discount the messages contained in our dreams, our reveries and our slips of the tongue. We simply laugh and classify them as silly or fanciful. Yet if we look more deeply at the symbols these messages bear, parts of our true selves begin to emerge. These are important pieces to include in your Soul Map.

If we remain receptive to these messages over time, we learn something important—that the unconscious mind is a deep source of wisdom and extraordinary insight.

THE MEANING OF DREAMS

HOW CAN we explore the subconscious mind and use it to connect more strongly with the true self? The most accessible place is in our dreams. We all dream, and most of us pause from time to time in the days after a significant dream to ask questions about it.

What did the dream mean? Why did my dream generate that unique story and those particular symbols? Why did my mind populate it with those particular people? What is the message for me, and what am I supposed to do about it?

Freud believed that dreams expressed deep-seated wishes, although disguised. Carl Jung believed that dreams contained universal symbols and archetypal patterns that bore significant messages for us. In their individual ways, both knew that understanding and respecting dreams gives us an important opportunity to understand our own unconscious, and to do our soul work. Dreams can offer a path to living a more authentic and congruent life.

Soul Mapping is mostly a conscious exercise, though designed in such a way as to invite input from the unconscious. In dreams, the unconscious has center stage, and often the messages for us are vital. A colleague believes that dreams on some level are trying to bring us "home" and asks clients to look for where the dream "tears" at you: How is it cleansing . . . or transforming . . . or nudging you in some new direction? Paying attention to your dreams moves you away from a sort of "autopilot" psychic life into one that is aware and can act on what you hear. Indeed, the whole Soul Mapping process is about paying attention to your inner life as it speaks and shifts.

INTERPRETING DREAMS

INTERPRETING DREAMS, fortunately, does not require the intervention of Freud or Jung. We each possess the needed abilities, if we take that first step of remembering our dreams and then subjecting them to a gentle investigative process in the days and weeks that follow.

Here is a dream described in KEN Ruge's book, *Where Do I Go From Here?*

KEN: George, my seminary roommate, found himself in the following context when he experienced his important dream. He was a first-year seminary student in New York, new to the city, and having doubts about whether he really wanted to be there. George was from rural Vermont and found New York to be a frightening, overwhelmingly difficult place to live. He did love a lot of things about city life, including the variety of interesting foods and the cultural diversity. But in our nightly bull sessions, he frequently questioned whether he should drop out of seminary and go back home, or stay in the big city and adjust.

George was studying the Bible at the time and was particularly engaged in the study of the Gospel of Mark, whose symbol, by the way, is the lion. One morning George woke me up at 6:00 A.M., excitedly telling me that he had just had a dream. In this dream, he found itself in his pajamas, standing on the corner of Broadway and 120th Street, trying to hail a cab. At that point, a very large lion came by. George somehow knew that he was supposed to ride the lion, so he got on and rode down Broadway about forty blocks to where a lot of people had assembled in front of Zabar's delicatessen. He was riding as if he were in the Rose Bowl Parade. He was riding along slowly in his pajamas, waving to the people as they cheered him.

In this very slow, long dream, George said he felt "regal, in charge, powerful." He felt that he and the lion were doing the right thing.

George's dream interpretation, which I think is the best, was that he should remain in New York and stay in seminary. He felt the dream was telling him he was doing the right thing in being here. It gave him a strong sense of the rightness of his decision and a certain reassurance that things would work out. He saw in this dream the support of his unconscious, whether symbolized by the lion or by the cheering crowd. And he also saw the dream's message that he could reign in this context, that is, feel in charge and be successful. When I asked George about the lion, he said that his associations to the symbol were courage, aggression, power, awe, and even God. Only later did it occur to him that he was studying the Gospel of Mark and that the lion was Mark's symbol.

SOUL MAPPING EXERCISE: DOCUMENT A DREAM

- ৡ∘ Record a dream you've had. Write it down and carry it with you for a day.
- ৡ∘ Sit down the next night and jot down what you associate with the dream. What comes to mind? What is your relationship to the words and symbols in the dream? What associations do they trigger? Write it all down.
- ৡ∘ Finally, evaluate the significance of the dream. What does it mean? Remember, you're the one who wrote the screenplay for this dream. What happened in it may be a wish on your part, or it may reflect where you are in your life. Given these considerations, how do you understand the meaning and significance of this particular dream? Is there any new life the dream is asking you to make room for?
- ৡ∘ Now take a moment with crayons or paints and draw a scene from your dream. Use the colors and the atmospheric feeling in it to express how you experience the dream. Add cut-out photos, sketches, etc. Save the drawing for possible inclusion in your final Soul Map.

REVERIES AND FANTASIES

LIKE DREAMS, our reveries and fantasies are products of our unconscious mind. They carry meaning and glimpses of our true self. They are important pieces to include in your Soul Map, since they can reflect your true motives and allow access to deeper levels of awareness. Through them, the unconscious mind offers a kind of confirmation or validation of our current life.

To access these glimpses, we offer two Soul Mapping exercises: winning the lottery and the observing ego.

WINNING THE LOTTERY

ONE OF the most popular fantasies in our culture today centers on winning the lottery or one of those sweepstakes that offer million-dollar prizes. One friend of ours says that she knows when she's feeling needy or frightened about something, because she starts fantasizing about winning the Publishers Clearinghouse Sweepstakes.

KEN: "I have another friend who regularly participates in the New York State Lottery. When I pointed out the minuscule chances of winning and tried to dissuade him, he cut me off abruptly and said, Wait a minute, Ken, isn't a dollar a small price to pay for a dream? I agreed with him and we moved on."

To be sure, the unconscious expresses itself in our daydreams, our fantasies and our reveries. It's important to listen to them and take them seriously, because they can confirm our choices and help us grow into a deeper understanding of our underlying motives and thoughts.

SOUL MAPPING EXERCISE: WINNING THE LOTTERY

- ❧ Taking the notion that "a dollar is a small price to pay for a dream," extend it: What would you do if you were told you had won the lottery?
- ❧ What would you change about your life? What would remain the same?
- ❧ Can you take this information about your dream and think of ways to integrate aspects of the dream now, without "winning?" What might these small, or not so small, steps be?

Another way to see what your unconscious is up is to track what you dream about during waking hours. Ask your ego to become observant of the reveries we all engage in every day.

SOUL MAPPING EXERCISE: THE OBSERVING EGO

- ❧ Build your "observing ego" by directing your conscious attention onto your obsessions and reveries. Where are you when you daydream? What's on your mind? What do you tend to think of over and over again? What reveries or fantasies do you have when you're sitting on a bus or just looking out a window?
- ❧ Take your "psychological pulse" two times during your daily reflection, jotting down recurrent thoughts, preoccupations, fantasies, feelings and inner songs.
- ❧ That same night, look over your notes and ask yourself what is going on in your inner life. What themes and deeper undercurrents occur?
- ❧ Do these themes and undercurrents connect with any of the other exercises in this chapter, or in other Soul Mapping chapters?

AWESOME ENCOUNTERS AND RESONANT SYMBOLS

ALL OF us have old photos we pull out from time to time. Maybe they are pictures of family, children, or our own childhood. What makes these photos important is that they are imbued with associations and meanings from the past. Each photo triggers certain memories and emotions. Keeping such photos honors and acknowledges the value of our own history.

Like photos, other objects in our lives become imbued with power and meaning as well. KEN: "My daughter Amanda has a teddy bear that she named Popsicle. Popsicle is imbued with enormous meaning for her and is her indispensable sleeping buddy. She speaks to Popsicle and apparently Popsicle speaks back to her. They have a relationship."

Donald Winnicott, the British psychoanalyst, would call Popsicle a transitional object. Winnicott has written that such objects help us move from connection with our mothers into eventual adulthood. We all have had such objects in our childhood that we endow with power and personal meaning.

Symbols produced by the unconscious mind are equally resonant with meaning, like the lion from George's dream. It's important to connect with such highly personal symbols, whether they are fleeting or central images in your personal history. By accepting ownership of the symbols that are unique to you, you honor your unconscious and, by extension, your true self. You let the unconscious know that you are tuned in and attentive to it, and to your own depths. By appropriating and reifying—that is, making concrete and objective—your symbols, you give them the opportunity to reveal their meaning and power over time. Through a gradual process of unfolding, the richness of your associations and personal images begins to emerge.

ARTFUL CHANCE ENCOUNTERS

NOT ALL the important personal symbols come to us in dreams and reveries. Some reveal themselves to us through new or seemingly chance encounters. KEN recently had such an experience at the Metropolitan Museum of Art in New York City:

"I found myself in the very last room of the galleries. As I turned and saw *Juan de Pareja*, a portrait by Diego Velasquez, I was stunned and transfixed by the intense gaze of the man who appears in the painting. The plaque next to the painting told me the story of the painting. Juan de Pareja was the artist's slave. Velasquez admired de Pareja, freed him in midlife, and then painted his portrait. The plaque said that when this painting was first displayed, reviewers in Rome said 'Some paintings are Beauty. This painting is Truth.'

"For me, the painting resonated with a sense of power and heroic courage that was palpable and moving. Something about my feelings for the painting transcended mere appreciation of it as art. I bought a postcard of it which I put in my son's room as a reminder of the importance of the symbol."

It's important to the Soul Mapping process to cultivate and maintain contact with a repertoire of personal symbols that carry meaning for you. Be aware of specific artworks, objects, experiences or people that strike you as vital, even if you don't know why at first. Attend to new symbols as they come to you in dreams and reveries, collecting them, as if in a basket, for your life and your identity. These things somehow resonate with your own true self. Keep these symbols in mind as you go about your daily life. Think of ways to keep them visible and vibrant. Understanding exactly what they mean is not the point, since their meaning may change and unfold over time. Keeping them accessible is the key.

SOUL MAPPING EXERCISE: COLLECT YOUR SYMBOLS

❧ Build a personal symbol collection. This process may entail several steps. Start by look-ing at old photos from the past. Which resonate for you particularly? What other sym-bols, whether from dreams, family, art, music, movies, your reading or your past rever-berate for you with meaning?

❧ Consciously bring all of these symbols and photos together in a collection. Then find ways to integrate those symbols into your life in ways that are enriching. You might hang them on the fridge door, put them in your office or carry them with you in your wallet, purse or pocket as a powerful reminder.

W O R D   A S   S Y M B O L

Don't be surprised if one of your "symbols" is a word that somehow grasps you at this time in your life. NINA remembers a pivotal college writing assignment for which the teacher asked the class to write an essay on a single word: "Out of nowhere came the word 'wanderlust.' Not a word I usually use, which was part of the point. Also out of nowhere came the entire essay, an outpouring on the strong associations I had with this word, associations that were unknown to me until this class brought them to the surface. The writing had a force all its own, and that lit-tle essay became the foundation of a professional life that embraced writing. To this day, 'wanderlust' remains a mysterious evocation—a reminder of parts of me that are still asking to be heard and integrated."

❧

RETURNING:
Mapping What You Find, Dreaming the Future

BY DOING the exercises in this chapter, you have surfaced some powerfully evoca-tive images, dreams and symbols. The temptation can be to relegate them to some sort of "fantastic" realm that has nothing to do with your daily life. That's why many of the exercises ask you to think of ways to integrate your exercise results into your life—if not literally, then metaphorically. Thinking about what you can do to appropriate *aspects* of what you have come up with in this chapter, recognizing that you may not be able to bring about a literal manifestation, is the work of "returning."

Many spiritual traditions assert the power of a genuine commitment to a course of action. Goethe, the great German thinker, spoke about how once we commit to something, then "Providence" moves too, and all sorts of events unfold to meet us. In the Soul Mapping process, we maintain that just *listening* to the symbols and responses that want to come out of you is the beginning of commitment to your deepest hopes.

From that commitment spring the topics of this section: synchronicity, and a greater ability to be awake, to perceive further promptings of your soul. Attending to all your "faint calls and small voices" increases their frequency.

TRACKING THE THEMES IN THE LONGING

IF "MAPPING what you find" has to do with commitment, how to commit to the faint calls? Start by simply acknowledging what you have heard so far. Honoring *all* your answers in this chapter is a way to invite them to be a part of your future. Images do require time to unfold. It's important not to dismiss them, however strange or irrelevant they may seem.

SOUL MAPPING EXERCISE:

- ❧ Go back to all your answers to this chapter's exercises: the dreams, the symbols, the secret lives, the fantasies. Re-read the introduction to this chapter to remind you of how vital your answers are.

- ❧ Record the themes, the images that seem most important to you. What is the message you most need to hear from these faint, or not so faint, calls? Since this chapter is very much about "angels knocking," you can jump to the Circle Page questions to zero in on what is pressing right now.

- ❧ List the ways you can incorporate the results of this chapter into your life.

PAY ATTENTION TO MEANINGFUL COINCIDENCES

AS YOU think of ways to incorporate this chapter's exercises into your life, don't be surprised if synchronicity makes an appearance. Synchronicity is the experience of meaningful coincidence. For example, you might be thinking about your dear friend in Hawaii, and just then he calls. Or you're talking to a group about your interest in insects and a butterfly inexplicably flies into the room, landing on your head. In such events, it is almost as though reality comes to meet you. The inner and outer worlds seem to touch.

In our rush to be productive and successful, many of us miss the richness of such meaningful coincidences. Yet if you can slow yourself down, even for a moment, you may better experience the texture, the irony, the humor, the upholding presence of meaningful coincidence.

Paintings of the Annunciation show Mary being addressed by an angel. We're told that Mary, when she was told she was to conceive a divine child, "pondered these things in her heart."

We also need time to ponder when we are interrupted by angels.

Who can explain the basis of a meaningful coincidence? Perhaps our inner intentions and dreams make us more aware of our corresponding surroundings. Perhaps something about our inner readiness draws a corresponding reality to us. Whatever the explanation, a meaningful coincidence can be a wake-up call, reminding us that reality can move with us, validate our experience, and confirm our dreams and hopes.

SOUL MAPPING EXERCISE: SYNCHRONICITY
—YOUR MEANINGFUL COINCIDENCES

- ❧ For the next couple of days, pay attention to any meaningful coincidences or unforeseen surprises that may occur in your life in the direction of a dream, an interest or a passion. Sit down and record in your journal any of these experiences that might have occurred:
- ❧ Have there been any experiences where you felt as though reality was confirming your choice or your interest?
- ❧ Are you feeling upheld in any ways by Providence in the direction you are moving?
- ❧ Have any surprising, unforeseen resources come to your aid, in ways that you didn't expect?

ૐ Now find a way to draw some of these experiences. How would you represent, through your drawing and your choice of color, Providence upholding you? Or Providence rising up to meet and aid you?

BEING FULLY AWAKE TO YOUR LIFE

ANOTHER SIGN that you are attending to calls in your life is the degree to which you are alive to the sensate world, the sights, sounds, touch, taste and aroma of your everyday life.

KEN gives an example from his practice: "In the divorce-recovery groups that I lead, most of the members go through a depression stage in grieving for their marriages. The world appears gray and colorless to people who are depressed. Their field of vision narrows. A beautiful blue sky is rarely noticed. All senses seem blunted and even the sense of time seems to slow. The sense of hope in the future seems to dim.

"As people go through the divorce process, they gradually move out of depression and begin the next stage: acceptance. They begin to wake up. They may begin to notice more in their lives: flowers blooming, the smell of pizza, the song of a bird. They wake up to the sensate world and come alive again."

What do we mean by waking up? Being awake means, among other things, being in your body, aware of your body. In his writings, Freud talks about "primary narcissism." This occurs when the baby is self-cathected—that is, when it is feeling empowered, connected and vibrant in its body. This kind of primary narcissism is important for us to carry with us into adult life.

We're not referring to selfishness or the kind of narcissism that puts us at the center of everything. This is a more basic, primitive, visceral self-connection. It's about the moments when you have a simple, pleasurable experience of being at home in your body. Feeling the sun on your face. Swallowing a cool drink on a hot day. Catching a glimpse of yourself in a store mirror and noticing yourself in a positive way.

These moments are about enjoying your world and enjoying yourself, but they involve your self-awareness in a vibrant context. It is as if you move from tunnel-vision to an endlessly broad vision of life. Your peripheral vision widens. Your awareness and concurrent appreciation of your immediate life ignites in a way that moves you to joy and gratitude. Like enjoying great music, waking up to this nonverbal, visceral experience offers an experience of grace.

Being wide awake carries with it an implicit feeling of gratitude for the world and for the invitation to share in its sensuous banquet of nature, our bodies and all God's creation. Look to the results of your exercises here for ways to experience new sensations, for a wider peripheral vision regarding who you are, and what is possible in your future.

SOUL MAPPING EXERCISE: INVOKING PRIMARY NARCISSISM

❧ Can you think of ways to exercise some primary narcissism at this point in your life? What can you do to enjoy being in your body? How can you involve the outdoors in this? The answer can be as simple and powerful as committing to a twenty-minute walk each day.

❧ Where do you need to widen your peripheral vision? What parts of your life are you missing by being too focused?

THE ETERNAL IN THE FLEETING

PARADOXICALLY, THAT which is fleeting can be the most insistent voice we need to hear at a given moment. It is the "still, small voice" that we hope for in times of transition, for it seems to know the way home. Trust your "faint calls and small voices" and, with humor and curiosity, resolve to see where they are leading you. You can start with turning to the Circle Page and continuing to listen to these mysterious sources within.

CIRCLE PAGE QUESTIONS

—❧—

YOUR CIRCLE PAGE:
What "Angels Are Knocking?"

LOOK OVER all you have written for this chapter. Think of it as a particular journey unto itself, into very specific territory. You return from this exploration with many thoughts and impressions. As a way to start that honing and honoring process, answer these questions quickly and intuitively. You can write directly in your circle or answer the questions on another piece of paper and then transfer the results to the Circle Page. Either way, this is a place to record the most insistent (and possibly most important) data from your responses; a place to capture the "angels knocking" at your door.

- Choose several colors and shapes that symbolize your "secret life." No one but you need know the meanings of these drawings.
- What childhood dreams, fantasies or longings can you re-capture? Add these phrases or images to your Soul Map circle.
- When you think of "escaping" your life, what images, places, qualities, or people come to mind?
- What dream images have you had? What recurrent symbols or characters or landscapes occur in your dreams?
- What insights or realizations have come to you as a result of doing the chapter exercises?

SACRED PLACE

OF ALL the answers to exercises in this chapter, which one(s) feel most sacred and important to you at this time in your life?

EMOTION

IS THERE a predominant emotion in your responses to the exercises?

SURPRISE

WHAT MOST surprised you about your responses in this chapter? What do you know now that you did not know before?

NURTURE AND RENEWAL

WHICH ANSWERS spoke the most to a hunger or a longing? Is there an aspect of your answers that, if it were more integrated in your life right now, would be particularly nurturing and helpful to you?

PERSONAL IMPERATIVE

AS YOU review your answers to this chapter, do you sense any imperative arising from what you wrote—any need to change your life? If so, where is the urge for change most insistent in this chapter?

DETOURS, LOSSES, CURVE BALLS, AND OTHER SURPRISES IN LIFE

"The right way to wholeness is through fitful starts and wrong turnings."

–C. G. Jung

GETTING THE LAY OF THE LAND

FAINT CALLS and small voices are one way the soul manifests itself, and as the last chapter pointed out, our challenge is to listen to them and somehow live out what we hear.

If the last chapter was about subtlety and its powers of transformation, this final mapping chapter is about all the inherently unsubtle whacks that come out of left field and elsewhere: the losses, surprises and detours that shape any life in crucial ways. As agents of change, they demand a place on your Soul Map, especially since their past effects often continue to shape present hopes.

This chapter is a place to chart some of the ways past detours and even seeming failures led to places you could not have gotten to otherwise. It is not so much a painful summary as a pulling together of things and people you have had to say good-bye to, as well as a look at the creative roles of inadvertence and disappointment. In the language of travel, this topic may seem like an unappealing destination. Why not just skip it? Since Soul Mapping as a process embraces the totality of our lives, our very *roundness*, losses and detours are not only part of the picture, but a source of power and insight for the future.

Ultimately, this chapter is a place to work on some of the unexpected ways change happens—an important part of a process designed to help people make conscious changes and embrace new directions.

Easing into unappealing territory

When someone asks us the perennial question, "How are you?" we like to answer, "Fine, thank you." And on some level, unless we are naturally fatalistic, we expect to remain "fine" indefinitely.

Our brains seem to be wired in the hopeful, naive way this response reflects, despite the capricious and often anguished nature of life and reality. Perhaps as a consequence of our habitually hopeful, buoyant outlook, we are often shockingly disappointed or genuinely surprised when life's predictable losses and detours occur. They remind us, suddenly, that we are not entirely in control of our world and our lives—that control itself is an illusion. As we live life we find that there is a precariousness in many of our most cherished areas: health, relationships, work, finances, and so on. Loved ones may die, or they may have died. Our marriage might dissolve or become troubled. We might lose our job. An important friendship might end. Good health might become bad. We might lose a home. Our hope and sense of a future can erode or disappear.

Of course, there are also surprising and seemingly positive detours in our lives, such as falling in love, being offered a job, winning the lottery, having a child, having a mystical experience or being forgiven.

As you examine this segment of your Soul Map, we invite you to look with new eyes at all such events: the losses, detours and surprises. Rather than seeing them as mere interruptions of bad or good luck, we encourage you to see them as an essential part of your life story and as events that carry meaning and perhaps even a message, urging you to move your life ahead in a certain direction.

On some level, we all know that the detours we encounter literally redirect our lives. They change us irrevocably. Even when the changes or losses feel unwelcome, they are a necessary part of who we are. In fact, losses and detours are a rich mine of learning and insight that ultimately call us into a new life. Let us begin by going back.

BEGINNING EXPLORATIONS:
Surveying the Past and the Present

THE LANGUAGE OF LOSS

EVERY FAMILY has grappled with loss and surprise over time. The question here is *how* people in your family greeted those experiences, and what stories and "truths" got attached to life's inevitable shifts.

Karen, for example, came from a small family; her only other sibling was a brother who had a lingering, life-threatening illness when he was a toddler. The experience affected her parents greatly, and while her brother recovered, some traces of the illness still persist in him. As a result of this experience, her parents have a well-honed, exaggerated tendency to worry. They tend to greet new developments in Karen's or her brother's life, whether positive or negative, with a "worst case scenario" response. This is a natural response, to be sure, rooted in the sudden nightmare of a deathly ill child while surrounded by friends with healthy children. But the *ongoing* nature of their response, while natural, isn't helpful—to them or to their children.

Loss has a life of its own, and can live on in the language of families, as well as in family philosophy and outlook. A dire view of change does not have to be rooted in tragedy, either; some family systems look upon *any* detour suspiciously, which can make it hard for family members to embrace or even seek out the surprises and detours so necessary to growth.

SOUL MAPPING EXERCISE: CHARTING THE UNEXPECTED IN CHILDHOOD

❧ Make a list of the unexpected events, either beneficial or tragic, from your childhood and adolescence. What happened? What were the results? What was the resolution, if any?

&2 Is there a **pattern** to the losses, detours and surprises that your family had to grapple with, and may still be grappling with? What constitutes a "loss" to you and to your family? For some, it could be the loss of a job, a divorce, or a death. In another family system, not getting into a certain school could be elevated to the level of tragedy.

&2 What narratives about the way life is emerged from these events? Did beliefs start to form like, "Things always go wrong?" "You can't count on anything?" What is your family's philosophy of change and surprise? Is surprise a teacher? Something to be embraced? Something to be avoided? Always tragic? Always suspicious?

&2 Think of ways, if any, that your family's childhood losses are still affecting your life today. Have you adopted any of your family system's past views of losses? Are they helpful to you or not? How might you modify the philosophy you grew up with?

THE DETOURS OF YOUR LIFE

TO THIS summary of past losses and surprises, we want to add a present-day example of the creative roles of disappointment and detours.

A friend participating in one of our divorce-recovery groups did the following Soul Mapping exercise, centering on her divorce as a major life detour. Although her divorce presented a very painful and unexpected loss, she discovered that it was a major life learning experience. Through it, she learned to be more assertive and expressive. She learned not to take love for granted, but to nurture and work at future relationships. She also realized that her judgment with regard to men needed to be examined, questioned, and revised.

Perhaps most importantly, she realized she needed to be an independent, self-defined woman who could support herself—even be content as a single person—and still want a committed, loving relationship.

As a result of her painful divorce, our friend suffered, grew, and redefined her life. Her loss initiated a process of change that resulted in a remarriage to a very different kind of man—not to mention a new lifestyle and a new perspective on life.

Death and resurrection represent a paradigm that is present in many of the great religions. It is also one of the most basic paradigms in nature and in our lives. Out of death, or ending, comes something new.

SOUL MAPPING EXERCISE: THINK OF A MAJOR CHANGE OR DETOUR IN YOUR LIFE

- Write a brief paragraph describing the detour. Perhaps it was the loss of a relationship, a death, a disappointment at work or some other major change. What happened? Who was there? How did you experience it at the time?
- Now go for a walk. Ponder those memories. Direct your mind towards those experiences.
- When you get back home, answer the following questions: What did you learn from this detour? What changes have occurred in your life internally and externally as a result of the detour? Have there been any positive results you can list? What events, experiences or relationships might not have happened if you had not gone through this detour? List some of the lessons you learned, however bizarre they might seem.

INVOKING THE POWER OF REDIRECTION

AFTER HAVING worked through a major past detour and reflecting on the results of it, take the loss and detour concept one step further: What do you need to let go of *now* in order to move on? How can you tap the power of detour and redirection at this point in your life? Not all losses are surprises, hurled at us when we least expect or want them. Some shifts are just waiting to happen more gently, if we will listen, and be on the lookout for them.

SOUL MAPPING EXERCISE: PULSE-TAKING EXERCISE—LOSSES ON THE HORIZON

- Take a look at the various areas of your life today: health, relationships, work, finances, friendships, family.
- What shifts are currently happening? Which ones can you sense on the horizon? What's opening up? What's closing down?
- What do you need to do to prepare for, engage, and work through these impending shifts?

TRAVELING DEEPER:
Charting New Territory

YOUR "BEGINNING explorations" in this chapter took you into deep territory rapidly, given the subject matter. To help you "chart" this territory, we invite you to explore a loss still unresolved, as well as look at where you might be in the whole cycle of grieving. Paradoxically, going deeper with this topic is the best way to ultimately surface from its depths, and to look toward a future informed by loss, not hostage to it.

WHERE ARE YOU IN THE LOSS CYCLE?

DESPITE THE obvious benefits of change, many people resist it. By refusing to accept a loss, some people can get trapped in grief, anger, and self-pity. According to psychologist Elizabeth Kubler-Ross, we go through a predictable series of emotional states dealing with loss. This can be true whether we're grieving a death, the loss of a relationship, or even a job.

According to Kubler-Ross, the expected stages of dealing with loss are:

1. *Shock and denial.* This state of consciousness occurs when we're first given the news of a loss. Often, we can't believe it's real. We don't want to think the loss has actually happened. We don't want to take in the information and the painful realization that our lives might change. Denial is probably the most primitive of all defenses. Like the ostrich, we bury our heads in the sand and say, "There is no problem. There is no danger. There is no challenge to my view of the world as it is."

2. *Anger* is next. Often, we're angry at a loss, or the death, or the change that's being presented to us. We want to lash out. We want to make it better, to bring back what we have lost. Above all, we resent having to go through the pain and the change that will inevitably ensue.

3. *Bargaining* is next—though it might occur either before or after anger. We believe that maybe, if we do or say the right thing, beg, or appeal, we can make things the way they were. Perhaps we really can return the toothpaste to the tube or arrange for that which has irrevocably changed to be

changed back. This outlook is related to magical thinking, in that we believe we can simply go back to "stage one" after we're further along.

4. *Depression* usually sets in once we realize that bargaining doesn't work. It's a state of mind in which our perceptual focus narrows. The world turns "gray." We tend to be less aware of what's happening in the world, more focused on our own pain and suffering. Often, we experience a loss of energy. With that comes lethargy, a feeling that we are simply living day to day and "getting by." Sometimes, we feel hopeless—as though this stage will never end and we will be stuck in a depression forever. This is because depression, by its very nature, prevents us from feeling hope or a sense of movement into the future. However, this stage does pass with time.

5. *Acceptance*, the next stage, begins to dawn gradually. Perhaps we wake up one morning and notice the blue sky. Or we experience a sudden sense of hope. At this stage, we're adjusting to the loss or change in our life. We're thinking that maybe we will be okay, maybe we really can move on.

These stages, of course, come and go. And with acceptance comes the final stage, which we would call "new life."

New life begins as we plan and see new options, possibilities, and lifestyles. At the same time, we begin the process of problem-solving and life-building. We're planning to move ahead, with a sense of hope and energy.

This is not a linear process; most people tend to work through these stages in a spiral fashion, moving back and forth. Perhaps you're finally feeling a sense of acceptance about a loss, then something happens to trigger your anger or depression again. For example, your ex-wife remarries. Or your deceased wife's friend calls, and you begin working through the problems all over again.

Recovery from loss, and acceptance of it, is a repetitive process that gradually leads into a solid state of acceptance, provided we can continue to feel our feelings and genuinely express our emotions about the loss or the change.

THE DANGER OF RESISTANCE TO CHANGE

WE CAN also get stuck in one or more of Kubler-Ross's emotional stages, and not move on. Any stage in the continuum, in fact, can become a working self-definition.

KEN relates some examples of this: "I once worked with an older divorced woman who felt 'abandoned and betrayed' by her ex-husband. She told me her story with such rage and contempt, I believed the events she was describing had occurred recently. Yet I learned that, in fact, her divorce had happened seventeen years earlier. The rage about her loss and her generalized anger at men were as fresh as if they had sprung to life only yesterday. Her identity had come to be defined by her loss—possibly forever afterwards.

"Likewise, I've seen widows, widowers and others who continue to see themselves as sad victims. My friend Gladys stated, 'God took away my Edward ten years ago, and I have never gotten over it.' Such people may view their continued grief and depression as a kind of loyalty towards the lost ones and as a way of honoring memory and past history. But that kind of outlook serves only as unresolved grief and results in a life that looks only backward."

Another danger in working through these stages of loss and detours can be generalization. We tend to create narratives and stories to help resolve our changes and our losses. But some stories are not helpful, because as generalizations, they are too broad and inclusive.

For example, Sally, who went through a painful divorce, wound up angrily generalizing that "All men are dishonest and angry." Therefore, she concluded she could never have another relationship, because "That's the way it is with men."

Likewise, Gladys, the friend mentioned above, felt she was never supposed to have a relationship again because God had given her only Edward, her deceased husband, and he had been the only person who could be close to her in her life.

Such generalizations about gender, or about God's singular intention, limit our lives and create a narrower, smaller, shrunken sense of the future. It is important to avoid them. Yet at the same time, we need to stress that such life stances are not unusual. All of us have some unresolved losses or detours we need to engage. They represent healing work that needs to be done.

SOUL MAPPING EXERCISE: ANALYZE AN UNRESOLVED PAST LOSS OF YOUR OWN

- ❧ Scan your life history and choose a loss that still feels poignant and unfinished.
- ❧ As you strive to select a loss to analyze, remember that some of the signature characteristics of unresolved grief are:

A reluctance and feeling of not wanting to deal with a particular past loss.

An idealization of the lost person, relationship, or job.

A sense of being haunted by the loss. It keeps coming up in various ways—in dreams, memories, and associations.

☙ Write about the loss you select, exploring what the lost person, relationship or other forfeiture meant to you.

☙ Consider where you might be in Kubler-Ross's emotional continuum, described above: Are you angry, sad, numb, hopeful, content? Have you really accepted the loss on a deep level?

☙ Consider doing this exercise for additional losses that seem unresolved. Collect and work on more than one. In the next section, we will explore some ways to bring resolution of these losses into your future.

FACING DEATH

LIKE A character in an Ingmar Bergman movie, death plays a role in each of our lives. We experience it first in childhood, with the death of a pet or an elderly relative. We are filled with questions, like those of KEN's youngest daughter, Amanda, who asked: "Why did Sparky, our fish, have to die? Where did his spirit go? When are you going to die, Dad? Am I going to die?"

We all have such questions, which we tend to put away as adults. We try as best we can to ignore the realities of death and the ephemeral nature of our time here on earth.

We believe fear of death is mostly about our fear of abandonment, of being left alone, one way or another. How we deal with the loss of someone close to us can affect our subsequent life trajectories.

Scott was the son of a very successful businessman who had made a great deal of money and had accumulated much power in his life. Scott was always in his father's shadow. When his father died of cancer several years ago, Scott felt sad, but also strangely liberated. There was no longer any shadow for him to be under. In a sense, Scott was on his own. This was both a scary place to be and an invigorating one.

SOUL MAPPING EXERCISE: ANALYZE THE DEATH OF A SIGNIFICANT PERSON IN YOUR LIFE

- Think of a significant person in your life who has died.
- Write the person's obituary from your perspective. Include in the obituary your description of your true relationship to the deceased. Elaborate on it.
- Consider how the deceased person's life influenced yours. What qualities and virtues have you gained through contact with this person? List them and then draw pictures about them, picking the appropriate colors to express your true feelings.
- Decide how this person's death influenced you, both for good or ill.
- Consider how your life trajectory shifted and changed after this person's death. Remember, we are both diminished and freed by the deaths of those we love.

CONGRATULATIONS, YOU'RE FIRED: CAREER DETOURS

SOMETIMES, THE "deaths" we grapple with are not physical, but the end of work we had come to rely on. The loss of a job or a career direction can be disorienting and scary. After all, most of us tend to go from day to day depending on a routine and a certain set of predictable expectations. When a job ends, the disruption that follows can throw our habitual life into chaos. But it is out of this chaos that change and new learning happens. We are forced to ask important questions, such as:

- "Why was I fired?"
- "What do I really want to do?"
- "Where do I go from here?"
- "What's my plan?"

The experience of being unemployed can give us the gestational time we need to explore our insights and/or life direction. Sometimes, the loss of a job can even be illuminating and helpful to us.

KEN: "My very first job was one summer during my college years. I was assigned to file magazine subscriptions in the basement of my college library. After only two days of this job, I felt miserable and confined in this windowless basement room during the beautiful days of summer. I was doing mundane clerical work for a small hourly wage.

"After three or four days, I started making errors in my alphabetization of the magazines. My supervisor noticed that I was making mistakes and, by the fourth or fifth day, I was asked whether perhaps this wasn't the job for me. In fact, I was asked to leave. I remember walking out that afternoon feeling devastated, ashamed and defeated that I had failed. Seven or eight days later, I actually felt relieved that I had lost the job and I started thinking of what other possibilities might be better for me. I finally found a job helping replace windows with the college custodian. I had a ball that summer and realized that work which is confining and clerical is not for me.

"If I had not lost that job, it might have taken me years to discover those realities. Sometimes, doors that close in your face offer the best learning experiences of all."

Collaborating in your job loss

One of the trickiest and most interesting threads to be aware of as you look at your work history is the degree to which you may or may not be a collaborator in your exits from various jobs. When unhappy in a situation, the soul has various ways to engineer exits, exits that sometimes can be quite disguised. But revealing them can move you from seeing yourself as a victim or failure at work to someone searching and trying to grow.

This is subtle business, easily misunderstood. We are not saying people are to blame for their loss of a job necessarily; sometimes a downsizing is just a downsizing, or a termination is patently unfair. There are other times, however, when we help engineer our own exits. NINA illustrates:

"In career counseling, I see many people whose unhappiness in a job they have long outgrown precedes their termination. They may profess surprise, even anguish at first, and these emotions are quite valid. They just aren't the only emotions operating. Eventually, many of these people admit the things they did at work to blow themselves out of the water, to guarantee that eventually something would have to give. It's as if there was no other way out except by this method of external loss, by this seeming corporate decision. But they were part of the decision all along, planting seeds that would ensure a change of scene."

SOUL MAPPING EXERCISE: ANALYZE YOUR VOCATIONAL PATH, DETOURS AND ALL

- Draw a timeline of your work life from adolescence until the present. Write each job you've held into the timeline and describe it.
- In which job were you the happiest? For what reasons?
- How did your jobs end? Were they losses you regret? Clear moves to something better? Did you engineer the move, or did it happen to you?
- If you were to move the timeline into the future—say the next ten years—what career, avocation or untapped potential would appear? Now try to draw that future. What color and shape would it take? What words or associations come to mind when you think of your vocational future? Use crayon and words to describe it.
- How might you move toward this vocational future? What concrete steps could you take now?

LOOKING FOR LIMITS: HONORING "WAY CLOSING"

PARKER PALMER, the educator and writer, likes to talk about the Quaker concept of "way opening" and "way closing." Way opening is when things seem to flow, to fall into place. You push on a door, and it opens. One thing leads to another. You are carried along, as if by an unseen hand.

Way closing, however, is another feeling altogether, yet just as directive and helpful. Your plans are thwarted. You pound on a door, and never get anywhere. Your best efforts are frustrated. It's as if the universe, or your soul, were trying to say: "Stop pushing in this direction. Just turn around and see what is beckoning over *there* . . ."

We also experience way closing when we come up against our limits, especially at work. We all have things we just can't, or don't want to do. But we're not taught to embrace our limits or be guided by them. Particularly in work settings, there is the assumption we will tackle anything that comes our way.

Yet our limits distinguish us, help us pick *this* type of work over that; this type of life over *that* one. Limits are the little bells that go off when someone describes a job to us that we don't want to do, but we feel we have to say yes anyway. Invariably, the job turns out badly, and we leave, one way or another. Limits move us from undifferentiated possibility into something more focused, more realistic, and truer to our soul's desire. When we run up against limits, when we experience way closing, they can be a marriage of inner and outer direction, pointing us home.

SOUL MAPPING EXERCISE: LOCATING YOUR LIMITS

- Recall times in your past when you bumped up against your limits, or when a "way closed" and things did not work out right for you.
- Were these experiences ultimately helpful and directive?
- Think of places in your personal or professional life now where you can feel the influence of your limits. Are you heeding or ignoring the message there? How can you use the discriminating power of your limits to further define your future in ways that work for you?

RETURNING:
Mapping What You Find, Dreaming the Future

FROM LOSS TO RESOLUTION

IT'S ONE thing to surface various losses and detours that may be unresolved and therefore still powerful forces in your life; it's quite another thing to engage them in ways that free you and your future. This is hard, essential, ongoing work. It is our hope that your Soul Map will hold the key places this work needs to happen, and that these exercises will move you toward resolution and acceptance.

SOUL MAPPING EXERCISE: RESOLVING LOSSES

- Refer back to the Soul Mapping exercise where you listed and analyzed unresolved past losses, especially losses involving people or relationships.
- Write a letter to the relevant person, even if he or she has passed away. State in this letter your feelings. Describe what this person meant to you. Where you are now with the relationship? How have you begun to put it behind you and move on? What do you think this other person's wishes for you might be?

- ☙ Visit the grave or the site of the loss. Walk around. Reflect on the loss experience. Give your mind some freedom to experience and to emote.
- ☙ Call a friend or relative who knows you well. Discuss the loss in some depth, face-to-face if possible.

This exercise helps us realize that it is important for us to move on in our lives and to allow ourselves to do so. Moving on does not mean forgetting a loved one or denying our past. We can never forget what was so important in our lives. Rather, moving on means putting our detours and losses in perspective, and allowing new people and opportunities to come into play in our lives.

SELF-ACCEPTANCE AND LONGEVITY

RECENTLY, A study was conducted of people who had lived beyond the age of 100. In this study of between 4,000 and 5,000 people, the researchers looked for common characteristics, or any characteristic that might explain how the study participants had managed to live so long.

Interestingly the researchers found virtually no common characteristic. Some of the participants drank, some of them ate too much, some of them had lived volatile personal lives while others hadn't. The only common characteristic the researchers could identify was that all of these people had been able to deal with, and grow beyond, the adversities and losses of life and come to some peace fairly quickly. They achieved a sense of peace and serenity and moved on. This may be a key for your own longevity and for your own future growth.

CULTIVATING PARADOX AND PERIPHERAL VISION

THE ABILITY to deal with and grow beyond loss is greatly aided by the tools of peripheral vision and paradox. The Bible is full of paradoxes, especially the injunction from Jesus that those who try to save their lives will lose them, and those who lose their lives will find them. Is this just a foolish or cruel saying? Not to a client named Mary; for her it was bedrock truth.

Mary was ensconced in a marriage that felt right, looked right, but was troubled by all that was unsaid. She got married fairly young; her course in life seemed pretty set, since her husband seemed to be a very stable guy. Unfortunately, he wasn't as stable as he seemed. Mary's world cracked apart in her late thirties, when her husband left her for another woman and moved overseas. This abrupt 180–degree turn launched her into a whole new life, painful in many ways, but eventually much more rewarding vocationally and personally. She used the time to learn—about herself, about theology, about training in a new field. She explained a few years later: "Did I *want* to lose my old life, and go through what I went through? Of course not. Do I no longer grieve the loss? No. I think it will always be with me. But it has been transformed into something larger than loss. It is utterly clear to me that only through this loss could my new life, which I love, have come. I don't pretend to understand this paradox, but I know I have to live into it."

WELCOMING SURPRISE

As Mary found out, the unexpected and the unplanned happen. In fact, they might make up the largest portion of our experience.

How we view the unexpected is all-important in how we will live our lives, and how much of our Soul Maps we will take in. After all, many of us cling to our old, preferred world view as a way to understand and define our experience. We discard or forget anything unexpected that does not fit neatly into that view. In this way we miss the boat. We can become blind to alternative visions and to the hand of God, which may be coming from the periphery, and to any voices coming from "left field."

Being *broadly aware* as we move through reality gives us more choices and chances to tap into the spirit's promptings. A broader view of reality also enriches us with the possibility of surprise and a promise of the unexpected, which can challenge and renew and enlarge our souls.

SOUL MAPPING EXERCISE: TRACING PARADOX AND SURPRISE

⊶ Look back over your life at the role paradox has played. Has any loss turned out to be a gain? Has any detour turned out to be just the direction you needed?

⊶ How do you view surprise, whether pleasant or troubling? Sometimes surprise comes as a way to widen our sense of what is possible, when it's clear we are not going to figure something out any other way. Think about your answers earlier in the chapter about how your family viewed loss and surprise. Is there a way you need to "step out" from past ways of viewing surprise?

❧ Look at the various aspects of your life—relationships, work, family, leisure time. Where is something new, waiting to break in? How can you anticipate and even participate in it? How can your put yourself more in surprise's path, and cultivate it?

"FOR EVERYTHING THAT HAS BEEN . . ."

NINA: "My paternal grandmother was very special to me, and one of her gifts to me was her favorite quote by Dag Hammarskjold, author of *Markings*. Initially, I thought it was a toast; now I believe it is a prayer. I think of it often:

"For everything that has been . . . *thanks*.

For everything that will be . . . *YES*."

This is a radical quote, urging us to respond to our "everythings"—all the losses, detours, curve balls and surprises—with a *thanks* for their formative power, and to look toward what is coming with a bold *yes*.

In that mysterious space between what has happened to us and how we *view* what has happened to us lies the soul's interpretation. That bold "yes" Hammarskjold urges does not come easily or cheaply: We all encounter fear in the face of change, and the next chapter will address the way that fear works in our lives. For now, move to the Circle Page with the questions below, and give your detours their place on the map. The Circle Page questions are designed to help you sift and hone and pull out the *essence* of this chapter for you. Feel free to add other questions of your own. You may find yourself adding new insights as you do so. Just let them come.

CIRCLE PAGE QUESTIONS

❧

YOUR CIRCLE PAGE:
What "Angels Are Knocking?"

LOOK OVER all you have written for this chapter. Think of it as a particular journey unto itself, into very specific territory. You return from this exploration with many thoughts and impressions. As a way to start that honing and honoring process, answer these questions quickly and intuitively. You can write directly in your circle or answer the questions on another piece of paper and then transfer the results to the Circle Page. Either way, this is a place to record the most insistent (and possibly most important) data from your responses; a place to capture the "angels knocking" at your door.

- List the big losses in your life.
- List some of the "life lessons" you have gathered.
- What losses are left undone, unresolved?
- What vocational changes have you experienced? What have you learned?
- List some "left field" experiences and encounters in your life. What did they lead to?

SACRED PLACE

OF ALL the answers to exercises in this chapter, which one(s) feel most sacred and important to you at this time in your life?

EMOTION

IS THERE a predominant emotion in your responses to the exercises?

SURPRISE

WHAT MOST surprised you about your responses in this chapter? What do you know now that you did not know before?

NURTURE AND RENEWAL

WHICH ANSWERS spoke the most to a hunger or a longing? Is there an aspect of your answers that, if it were more integrated in your life right now, would be particularly nurturing and helpful to you?

PERSONAL IMPERATIVE

AS YOU review your answers to this chapter, do you sense any imperative arising from what you wrote—any need to change your life? If so, where is the urge for change most insistent in this chapter?

PART TWO

LIVING
YOUR
SOUL MAP

How to integrate and implement
the results of this book's exercises

11

WHAT'S IN THE WAY
FEARS, DOUBTS, AND OTHER ROADBLOCKS

———— ❧ ————

"If you want to identify me, ask me not where I live, or what I like to eat,

or how I comb my hair, but ask me what I am living for, in detail, and

ask me what I think is keeping me from living fully for the thing I want

to live for."

—Thomas Merton

Congratulations. . . . Whether you have done one Soul Map chapter or all of them, you have spent time listening deeply to yourself, creating from your unconscious, and thinking about what has shaped you thus far in your life and where you want to go from here.

So now you're ready to speed into the chapters on reading your map as a whole and applying it to your life. Or maybe not.

We feel this book would be incomplete to the point of being deceptive if there were not, right at this point in the process, a practical acknowledgment of all that gets in the way of working with the results of Soul Mapping: the fears, the resistances, the excellent objections. The reasonable procrastination. The roadblocks both internal and external. To ignore these gremlins is both foolish and unrealistic. To honor them *too* much leads to stasis and frustration.

Our purpose in this chapter is to help you uncover what is in the way—to name both the obvious and subtle barriers that can hinder putting your Soul Map to work. Without this chapter, the power of the Soul Mapping technique can be too easy to ignore, because nothing brings out more fearful voices than the possibility that we might *actually change*, that we might do things differently! So at the very point where your Soul Map may be revealing new possibilities to you—*that's* the signal to the inner defenders of the status quo that they need to go on high alert. As Abraham Maslow put it, "Fear of knowing is very deeply a fear of doing."

SOUL MAPPING AND FEARS GO HAND IN HAND

THE VERY nature of the Soul Mapping process invites the new . . . and invites the fears that naturally accompany the new. The process is open-ended; you don't know what you will come up with. While the chapters have topics, unlike many self-help books each chapter's "agenda" is you—what you bring to the map, and what in your psyche needs to be heard.

So the Soul Mapping process is very much a *pilgrimage*, with all the tensions of that word: Pilgrims set out, not knowing where they will be led. Their journeys can be long, arduous, confusing, revealing, joyous and confirming all at once.

Many of these journeys involve a bridge, either literal or internal: a place where you are forced to stop. You can see what's beckoning ahead of you, but something needs to get you from *here* to *there*. You have to cross the water, bridge the distance between stopping place and destination.

Roadblocks and fears can force you to stop and assess; engaging what stops you can act as the bridge. The exercises in this chapter are bridges at heart. They help you:

1. Identify the things that are stopping you, whether large or small, and
2. Engage and counter those things creatively and constructively.

Work through these exercises with the fruits of your Soul Map exercises and you will be very prepared to move into the chapters that follow.

ENLARGEMENT IS AT THE HEART OF THE PROCESS

SOME OF the exercises in the "Capturing Today" chapter asked you to reflect on where *enlargement* was at work in your life—where were you being pushed outside various boxes and invited to stretch?

At its core, the Soul Mapping process is about seeing yourself as *bigger*. Part of the Today chapter gets at this explicitly, but the rest of the book traffics in enlargement, too. Seeing childhood with a wide lens . . . giving yourself permission to brainstorm a future that includes things envied and desired . . . the important "parts" of yourself that surface in hobbies and travel plans . . . Soul Mapping invites so many parts to surface that the whole becomes large indeed. Perhaps larger than we remember—or believe.

To let in the sense that you, your talents, and your future possibilities are larger than you previously thought inevitably ushers in change. Even if it is "only" a change in your perception of yourself and what is possible, it is a shift nonetheless. And that shift will have a cost.

Soul Mapping broadens identities, and the first roadblock can be sheer immobility. A refusal to know or do the thing we are called to do—because we will have to change. That change can mean leaving behind what is safe and familiar. This kicks in our most basic defense in the face of what we know we need to do: procrastination. At its most subtle, procrastination can manifest as carefulness, or the sense we are doing something, when in fact we are steeped in delay.

If it's true that fear is one of our most powerful emotions, and we structure our life around avoiding it, then resistance to change becomes a hallmark of fear. We sense the impending loss, and we turn the other way. As the old saying goes, we prefer known hells to unknown heavens.

Author Ann Ulanov once described the goal of spiritual direction as "trying to free people to accept the heat." To the degree to which Soul Mapping is a spiritual direction tool that helps you *listen* to what is happening in your life, can it also help free you to "accept the heat?" We think so, and one way it can is to help you zero in on where the call to be "bigger" is showing up. It can be a subtle call, with many guises:

FEAR'S STARTING PLACE:
THE MANY GUISES OF THE CALL TO BE "BIGGER"

IN MANY instances, your reaction to what comes up in a Soul Map is *not* surprise; the maps can confirm, support, or summarize what you already know. But they can also reveal the first intimations of something that may have to change—of ways growth is at work.

WHERE THE *RESTLESSNESS* IS.

Look at the results of all the Soul Mapping exercises for dissatisfaction, even frustration. Restlessness is a natural result of a growth cycle, and can be a call to the new. Have you outgrown something? Are you longing or yearning for something? Are you wrestling with something?

Where are you called to go beyond a comfort zone? Where is the world calling you to come out of hiding?

WHERE THE *TENSION* IS.

The next chapter on reading your map whole will say more about the usefulness of locating tensions, but a quick scan is good here, as a way to locate places of discomfort and therefore potential. The tension could be between something old and something new, something trying to be born and something that has to die. The soul is at work in these cracks.

Especially look for the things that "don't fit" on your map: the opposites that contradict each other; the pieces that don't fit together.

For example: a passion for being in the outdoors and a current life that doesn't allow for it; a love for a certain academic subject and a childhood sense that you wouldn't do well if you went back to school; a very extroverted fantasy life and a quiet, introverted persona, etc.

The things that don't fit in your Soul Map are not exercises in frustration; they are clues as to how *wide* your sense of self needs to be to accommodate them all. Rather than banish conflicting elements to the basement, or deem them inappropriate, Soul Mapping invites you to listen to and integrate them.

WHERE THE *PROCRASTINATION* IS.

The poet David Whyte once observed there is nothing more frightening than finally finishing your studio—because then you would have to paint. Soul Maps are good tools for locating where you are procrastinating: where there are things you really want to do and are not doing them. One way procrastination shows up down the road is in "deferring the dream"—having a vague dream that never gets acted on or even explored. We then live with a vague sense of disappointment or depression.

Look at your own procrastination patterns and see the many ways it shows up. Look especially for that common procrastination disguise: ambivalence.

WHERE THE *AMBIVALENCE* IS.

Looking for the internal roadblocks on your map brings up a basic paradox—that which we most desire, we also avoid. Rudolf Otto made the famous observation that in spiritual traditions we are always attracted *and* repelled by the holy or numinous. The same might be said of your Map results. As a creative expression of what is deeply important to you, it is a holy document. And you may want to turn away from its gifts. In ancient Greece, the touch of a god was a blessing and a violation at the same time, for it tore you out of your old world.

Soul Mapping is not necessarily that violent, but it does raise basic questions about intention and stewardship of time. David Whyte once said something in a lecture about poetry that applies perfectly to Soul Mapping: "A good poem will frighten you, kill you, humiliate you—return you to the center of your being and make you ask: 'how much of your life are you living firsthand?' "

"Living firsthand" is a key goal of the Soul Mapping process. So as various chapters ask you to stretch your sense of what is possible or appropriate, let's look at the specific fears and reactions that can arise.

IDENTIFYING FEARS: LARGE, SMALL, AND HIDDEN

FEARS, OFTEN appearing as roadblocks, rationalizations, etc., can be strewn across many a Soul Map. They can show up as large, global issues, or can be cleverly hidden—like a way of being in the world that is subtly unhelpful to you.

The issues underpinning the fears can be large indeed:

FIRST, THERE'S DEATH.

The "death" involved in any choice, commitment, or the decision to take on an identity can keep people from committing in the first place. Choose one path, the others are automatically negated or lost. Yogi Berra was fond of saying, "When you get to the fork in the road . . . take it!" This is awfully tempting—to try to go down two roads at once, no decision required. Keep your options open. But eventually, options never exercised expire.

SECOND, YOU MIGHT BE BETRAYING THE FAMILY.

Many people get stymied by longings embedded in their Soul Maps because a small voice inside says, "If I do this thing, I will violate an unconscious hidden loyalty." Breaking out of old patterns may seem appealing, but unconsciously the worry lurks: move beyond the family system and you're lost.

THIRD, IT'S EASIER TO BETRAY YOURSELF.

In a Bible story so grim it's often abbreviated or skipped over during the Christmas holidays, King Herod, informed of Jesus' birth, wants this new and possibly powerful being killed so badly that he orders the slaughter of thousands of baby boys. Putting aside our own backgrounds of faith, this disturbing story asks everyone: How is this a story in our lives? How do we set out to destroy the redemptive thing that has appeared in our midst? How do we greet the new in our lives? When even chronic procrastination seems too risky, since something new may eventually occur, we resort to squelching, to killing off the new impulse, often in the name of prudence. As fear crops up in your responses to your maps, take care not to squelch what is trying to be born.

"SLAPPING DOWN THE UNCANNY"

On some level, we can all have Herod energy, and it can masquerade as decisiveness, order, and rightness. Swift judgments. Little humor. As renowned Jungian analyst Marie Louise von Franz observed during an interview, "When, during life, we are assaulted by new parts of ourselves, we reject them. We slap down the uncanny."

When something new comes up from the psyche (and the Soul Map is very much a tool for bringing this material up), we may greet it with sabotage. Or we may simply flee. This isn't just perversity, but an old prehistoric survival mechanism: Greeting with suspicion or rejection the thing that doesn't fit is essential when enemies or wild beasts make up your world. But it moves from healthy perception of danger to neurosis when there is no tiger.

How to counter the "Herod energy" that fears the new? Try the opposite responses: welcoming; questioning; humor. Try suspending decisions about what's right until you've worked with what has come up on your map, especially using the last two chapters of this book.

The philosopher Søren Kierkegaard coined a wonderful phrase: *"The alarming possibility of being able."* Soul Mapping brings up all *sorts* of possibilities. Try to identify where the alarm lurks.

SOUL MAPPING EXERCISE: FEAR CANVASSING

ᵭ Look over your answers to the exercises in the **Returning: Mapping What You Find**, **Dreaming the Future** sections of all the Soul Mapping chapters. Because these sections ask you to look forward, and think of ways to integrate what's coming up into your life, fear will crop up here first.

ᵭ Make a list of all the fears that accompany the desires and hopes that manifest in your exercises.

ᵭ Working with this list and the above sections on ambivalence, tension, restlessness, procrastination, and King Herod too, make a list of the current fears in your life now. Are there patterns? Does one predominate? For an interesting addition, ask a good friend what **they** see as the thing you are most afraid of. Just floating these to the surface, acknowledging, and naming them is the first step to moving beyond them.

FEAR'S SUBTLE MANIFESTATIONS

OTHER ROADBLOCKS to directions Soul Maps point at are very subtle. At their root fear also lurks, but it expresses itself in quietly persuasive ways:

DEFLECTIONS AND CONTINGENCIES.

We can convincingly stall ourselves in what author James Hollis (see Resource section) has uncomfortably called "all the subtle deflections of personal responsibility." Contingency language starts to creep in: "If only *this* would happen . . . *then* I would do that." "Yes, of course that's important to me . . . *but* . . ." "When this outcome happens, *then* I'll do what I need to do." These comfy phrases can be the foundation for an in-between, not-yet life, one that is provisional and contingent. These phrases sound *safe*; they are hard to argue with. So it's important to see where they are lurking, and whether they are about legitimate obstacles or not.

RESISTANCE TO OPPOSITES.

Sometimes Soul Mapping floats up contrary desires—situations where elements are seemingly locked in opposition. Aspects of "today" may be at odds with hidden desires; hopes for the future may not fit with past education, etc. When these tensions pop up, resisting, ignoring or dismissing them are common initial reactions. Try to see them not as impossibilities but as elements in dialogue, aspects of you that can, with some engagement and wrestling, be integrated or lead to a third way of doing things. It's through precisely this kind of conflict that newness comes in.

LINEAR LOGIC.

One thing that can stop change in its tracks is to let preconceived notions of timing hold sway. You may have a lot of enthusiasm about the result of a Soul Mapping exercise. The new direction may involve some change, but you are excited. Then the little voice says, "It's too late." Or "You're too old." Or "It will take too long." So the energy goes back down. We can easily get caught up in a worry about time that is linear or ruled by a sense of scarcity. As with the "yes, buts" it's important to look closely at these objections to determine how legitimate they are. (Hint: When these objections come up, counter them by looking for exceptions to the rule: the aunt who switched careers at age 62; the friend who went back to school despite financial contraints; the colleague who broke into the field without credentials, etc.)

SOUL MAPPING EXERCISE: LISTING THE "NOT-YETS," AND THE "YES, BUTS . . ."

When we're trying to make changes, a part of us wants to shift; a part is made very nervous by the prospect.

ॐ Look over your summary pages and jot down any deflections you see. What are your current "yes, buts" and "not yets" and "if onlys" that are in the way of whatever desires, needed movement, new directions, etc. you feel are calling you?

ॐ How can you engage and challenge them? Parker Palmer captures the dilemma—and the opportunity—when he says: "It means giving up the comfort of what Marie-Louise von Franz calls 'the not yet.' As long as I can go on convincing myself that this is not the time, that this is not the place, that I haven't yet arrived, I can always slip out of a difficult situation and make my pilgrimage an excuse for moving on. I do not want any form of closure or finality, because I would prefer the fantasy that sometime in the future the real thing will come about."

How to move beyond these seemingly safe but actually very costly "not yets?" Start by jumping into the exercises that follow.

WAYS TO ENGAGE AND COUNTER YOUR FEARS

IN THE last lines of her poem "When Death Comes," Mary Oliver writes about the importance of desiring and pursuing amazement, about coming to the end of her life and not having to wonder if she made something "particular" and "real" with the time given her. The poem ends with her saying, "I don't want to end up simply having visited this world."

This powerful poem asks us to receive and embrace the full range of what life offers. Your completed Soul Map is an ideal place to start. And it presents the same two choices that faced the poet: You can *engage* your map . . . or you can just *visit* it. Fear will urge you to just pay respectful visits. How to engage instead? Here are some thoughts:

LEARN TO RECEIVE

Fears and roadblocks crop up in the Soul Mapping process; this is a given. They won't go away; indeed, the more you engage this process, the more they engage you. So how to welcome them and work with them?

One clue is in the poem above: it advocates a type of receptivity regarding the gifts from the world to you. We think "receptive amazement" is the ideal stance to take with your overall Soul Map. Let in what it says; take it seriously. The next chapter will help you "read" and therefore receive it in a variety of ways— metaphorically as well as literally.

LEARN TO MOVE TOWARD THE FEAR

In his book *The Active Life*, Parker Palmer writes about being stuck on a deadly ledge in the midst of an Outward Bound course. As he contemplated never moving again, the instructor way down on the ground yelled up that this might be a good time to reveal the Outward Bound motto: "If you can't get out of it, get into it." At first he was annoyed at this advice, but then he wrote:

"Bone-deep I knew that there was no way out of this situation except to go deeper into it, and with that knowledge my feet began to move."

Carl Jung often pointed out that the greatest opportunity for personal growth is what most frightens you. There is an aspect of *treasure* here.

SOUL MAPPING EXERCISE:

❧ Look at your list of fears so far and write down what moving *into* them would look like.

DIALOGUE WITH THE FEAR

Uncovered fears are valuable for the wisdom they hold. Hesitancies have a kernel of truth; objections can be a blend of legitimate danger and veiled excuses. Trying to banish fear won't work, and leads to self-sabotage, especially if you haven't received whatever legitimate message is embedded in the fear.

What's the gift or hint within each fear you're facing? What is it trying to tell you? One way to get at this message is to do a simple journaling dialogue with the fear:

SOUL MAPPING EXERCISE: DIALOGUING WITH FEAR

❧ Pick a fear from your list you want to work with. Write a dialogue:

> (**Your name**): you ask the fear a question; you address it.

> **Fear of** _____: Just see what comes up as you write. Continue to go back and forth in dialogue. The results can be very surprising.

For example, Wendy is a client who would like to step off the fast track for a year or so, and do something completely different, based on some input from her Soul Map. Fear blocks her. Here is what she wrote:

> Wendy: What are you? Why do you keep me stuck?
>> Fear of leaving the job: I am scarcity. I am realism. If you leave the loop now, you'll never get back. Other people will take your place.
> Wendy: But I'm not happy in the loop.
>> Fear: I don't care. We're safe.
> Wendy: We're not just safe . . . we're scared for the wrong reasons.
>> Fear: That's what you think. I pay the rent.
> Wendy: That's true—what else do you do?
>> Fear: I give you approval; you don't have to explain yourself to your parents, or to anyone else. What you do makes sense.
> Wendy: But it doesn't make me happy.
>> Fear: That's not my problem. It's yours.
> Wendy: Tell me more. . . .

Wendy went on with this "dialogue" and followed the fear down to its bedrock place of parental and societal approval. Once there, she could shine a light on it and work **with** it to let some changes into her life. She offered the following observations. "This exercise seemed silly at first, seemed like 'pretend.' But I was amazed at how quickly the fear spoke back, immediately and snappishly. Yes, I was technically writing for both sides, but the fear part had a voice all its own and was just waiting to be invited to speak. I got information I could not have gotten otherwise."

The point of this exercise is to let the fear be *heard*, and give you a chance to use whatever helpful observation the fear needs to convey. This is integrative work: Not ignoring fear heedlessly, and not getting stuck in it, either—but engaging it, learning from it and using it to move forward.

DO THE WRESTLING AND SORTING

Beyond identifying and then dialoging with fears lies the need to sort them. To separate out what's real and what isn't. To try to determine what is from us, what is from the culture, what is from our families, etc. If psychologically, we experience the things that bring us to consciousness as forms of betrayal (betrayal of the past, the status quo, our sense of self, the family, etc.), then *engaged* wrestling with these things is essential if we are to see the growth embedded in the fear, and the blessing amidst the betrayal.

FIND THE FREEDOM TO FAIL

It may sound odd, but failure is essential to working with your Soul Map. Think of "failure" as part of stepping out and trying something new—as simple input and direction, not as an evaluation of your character. Failure as unavoidable. We need the freedom to fail, especially as adults. The alternative is perfectionism, and a fear of mistakes that will keep you trapped in possibility and contingency.

A client who works in advertising has a wonderful perspective on failure at work. He is a smart, creative writer who, as he puts it, fails all the time; it's part of the job. For any given ad, he has to come up with 10–12 concepts, and the client will only pick one. The rest ostensibly "fail." But not for the writer. He makes sure they are all good, enjoys doing them, and knows this is a subjective business. And it's his playfulness, and freedom, and knowing it's in doing them all that one "succeeds" that he grows as an artist.

PRACTICE LEADING THROUGH FEAR

Fear can be a catalyst for growth, especially if you focus on your goal—what you want—instead of on the fear.

Identify current fears, especially regarding actions you may need to take. Can you put them in the following format, and thus shift the emphasis to the goal?

FEAR	GOAL	ACTION

For example, you may want to do a large, creative project like write a book. The fear could be that you're not good enough, you can't write that much, you don't have time, and so forth. Fine—write all the objections down. Then write down the goal despite the fear: finished manuscript by a certain date, etc. Looking at the *goal*, not the fear, what action do you need to take? It could be one chapter every month; start research on topics, research on publishers, etc. Then pay attention to the action column as you go forward.

TAKE THE TOKEN STEP

Don't worry about starting small; the action steps you list above can be small ones indeed. This method is also a key antidote to procrastination—to break down even the biggest project into the smallest steps; to "eat the elephant one bite at a time." In doing so you begin to move from comfort zone into capacity. It's fearful, yes . . . and precisely the type of small, forward movement that helps fears diminish. And the step does not have to be into clarity: Spiritual wisdom says often the first step . . . is to get lost.

DISTINGUISH KAIROS AND CHRONOS

The Greeks had two words for time. "Chronos" was for the handy linear sense of time that keeps us "on time": it governs calendars, watches, train tables and other efficient devices. "Kairos," however, translates as "God's time" or "fullness of time." It refers to the gestational, circular, organic ways things happen. Taking action in ways urged by your maps will most likely happen in kairos time. We tend to think change needs to occur by a certain time, when the process is far more incremental and mysterious than any schedule.

REMEMBER THE POSSIBILITY OF PRAYER

It would be hard for us to include a checklist on how to deal with fear without mentioning prayer, whatever your religious persuasion. We spoke about prayer in the "Envy" chapter, and it's even more pertinent here. You can bring prayer into your frustrations, hopes and worries regarding your Soul Map. Tell God your fears about going forward. Try that in a journaling format. Sometimes we get the power we need to respond to a call, but only after we take the first step.

Soul Mapping is a mysterious process that invites participation from our true Self. You are not alone in this enterprise, and prayer, whatever its form, can bring to mind the Other which is always there.

FEAR AS A NATURAL PART OF THE PROCESS

HERE ARE some final notes on fear as you go forward into working with your map as a whole. We came across a quote recently that we have been using in our workshops. Jean Paul Sartre said this to his friend Albert Camus:

> In order to remain yourself, you should have changed . . . but you were afraid to change.

Sartre captures the paradox at the center of the Soul Mapping process and at the center of any personal journey: Change is essential for us to "remain" ourselves, and yet we fear it.

Carl Jung wrote of how every mid-life crisis was a spiritual crisis, where we are called to die to the ego, or old self, and liberate the new man or woman within us. He thought that we experience every advance for the self as a defeat for the ego.

In other words, your fears are essential and unavoidable. They invite your participation. Indeed, they are pointing the way.

PUTTING IT ALL TOGETHER
VIEWING YOUR SOUL MAP AS A WHOLE

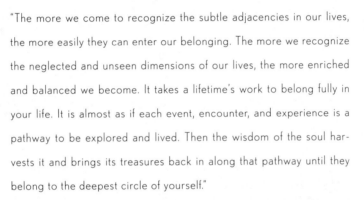

"The more we come to recognize the subtle adjacencies in our lives, the more easily they can enter our belonging. The more we recognize the neglected and unseen dimensions of our lives, the more enriched and balanced we become. It takes a lifetime's work to belong fully in your life. It is almost as if each event, encounter, and experience is a pathway to be explored and lived. Then the wisdom of the soul harvests it and brings its treasures back in along that pathway until they belong to the deepest circle of yourself."

–John O'Donohue, *Eternal Echoes:*
Exploring Our Yearning to Belong

INTRODUCTION

THOMAS MERTON once made a powerful, challenging distinction with these images: A bird calls, announcing the difference between heaven and hell. Heaven is our capacity to hear the bird. Hell is not hearing the call at all.

Soul Mapping, as these many chapters have pointed out, is about deep listening. And while we don't want to make "heaven" and "hell" distinctions between our differing abilities to listen to our maps, Merton's declaration reminds us of the sheer importance of being *present*—with open ears, eyes, and heart.

Each chapter of this book tries to help you open to a particular topic in your life; what happens when you put them together? How should you read the results of the "Childhood," "Envy," and "Culture" chapters as they jostle and contradict each other? Do the little pictures and glimpses from chapters add up to a big picture? How do you know what's most vital from what you have floated up?

This chapter will help you to answer these questions and more. It will give you various ways to see how all the parts fit together and honor each other, a way to see the forest and the trees. We will describe how to let the chapters "talk" to each other, even if they disagree. Part of this chapter is logistical—how to assemble the Soul Map. But most of it is philosophical and spiritual. Reading your map in its entirety is an exercise in mystery. Some answers will come in whispers; some in shouts. To get at some of these answers, we will continue to use some exercises in the form of questions.

The goal of the entire Soul Mapping process is to live in *relationship* to your map's contents. Ideally this relationship becomes a real partnership, as you live and work with all the parts of yourself.

The odds are your maps have produced many of the "subtle adjacencies" the above quote speaks of. This chapter will help you recognize the messages they hold.

FIRST, THE LOGISTICS

THE PHILOSOPHY of "no right or wrong way to do a Soul Map" carries through to the assembly part. You can do any or all of the following steps. As a data gathering process, Soul Mapping starts wide and gets narrower:

1. First, you work on individual chapters, where different exercises help you gather a lot of personal, creative reactions and ideas.
2. Then you are asked to *summarize* each chapter's fruits on the circle pages that become your overall map. You don't lose your initial reactions; you hone and summarize them for easy reference.
3. On the circle pages, you can add images, color, shapes, pictures, etc. These circle pages represent a personal vocabulary of your inner world, whether you used word, symbol, color, feeling, event, etc.
4. You can then take the completed circle pages and put them together into your large Soul Map. Fix them in place or move them around. See which need to be next to others. See how they overlap or disagree (more on this later). Read the circles separately and together; see what shifts. You now

have the classic "bird's-eye-view" of your life. Knowing how to take it all in starts with the imperative of receiving it in the first place.

RECEIVING THE WHOLE OF YOUR MAP

NINA RECALLS: For various unexpected reasons, I found myself back in the Episcopal church in my late 30s, active in worship and education. One summer Sunday, I was in a small church on Long Island where I knew no one. Alone in my pew, I was mulling over something as Communion was being prepared. Quietly, the usher appeared at my pew and asked a simple, procedural question: "Do you wish to receive?" I had never heard this before in a service. It wasn't just logistics, or a signal to walk toward the altar; it was an *invitation*. Simple enough: Sure, I had planned to go up for the bread and wine, as always, but as I stood up, prompted by those words, the tears came all at once.

In my surprise, I realized the question was huge: Do I wish to receive? Can I take grace in? Is all of me up there at the Communion rail? How do I hide? How do I deflect? How do I *not* receive?

Looking at your Soul Map—in parts or whole—asks the very same question: "Do you wish to receive?" Can you take in the sheer glory of it, in its wideness, its contradictions, its improbabilities? Are you a "stingy" receiver? Carl Jung has said that we are born millionaires, but most of us live like paupers. You are not a lone, single story; reading your map whole tells you that. It takes you into the realm of what author and professor Barry Ulanov has called "feeling the drunkenness of things being various."

Our rampant "variousness" jumps out when we look at our maps whole, as a big picture. It can be tempting to tidy things up, either out of efficiency ("that's just not practical") or despair ("Who am I kidding? I'll never be able to do that"). Shaping the variousness, owning and honoring it, is the next step in the Soul Mapping process. Here are two basic ways:

REFRAIN FROM JUDGING

One of the swiftest ways to not receive the new, or the longed-for, from a Soul Map is to judge it. Just as working with last night's dream requires you to stay with its mysterious images long enough to think about what they might be saying to you, images and ideas from a Soul Map need "dwelling time." They need you to suspend disbelief a bit, to have fun with even the seemingly absurd. Discernment—a keen awareness of whatever truth lies in your maps—is different from judgment, which is quick to evaluate and dismiss.

Yes, some weeding of your map results is necessary, but initially, just let everything in. Let your first response to your maps be welcoming.

ACCEPT YOUR OWN AUTHORITY

As a technique, Soul Mapping embodies the true meaning of the word education. In Latin, *educare* means to lead out of . . . to draw out of people what they already know. That's very different from an outer "authority" pouring knowledge into you. Your dreams, your unconscious, and your images are your sources of authority.

You did the exercises, drew the maps, floated up the images. Some are imperative to you for reasons only you know. The "authority" to interpret or act on what you came up with is already contained—in you. Clarissa Pinkola Estes writes about how being strong means to meet our "own numinosity without fleeing." Doing this rests on an assumption outlined in the "Capturing Today" chapter: that Soul Mapping is connected with the practice of spiritual direction; that it traffics in "continuous annunciation."

YOUR MAP AS A SPIRITUAL DIRECTOR

THINKING OF your map as a large exercise in spiritual direction is not about creed, or dogma, or whether you go to church, or any of the trappings of traditional religion. It's larger than that. The spiritual direction approach to your map means asking: What is God saying to me in this map? What do I need to be open to? To listen to? To act on? Where is the "still, small voice" I most need to hear now?

REDEFINING "RELIGION"

WE SAID Soul Mapping is "educational." We also need to say it is "religious" in the true sense of the word. *Religiare* means to tie or re-bind together. Unfortunately, "religion" has come to have connotations of doctrine, rule-following, uninspiring church services, bad childhood memories. But the root word has very different ideas; like Soul Mapping, it encourages a tying together, an honoring of all the parts, and an integrating into a new whole.

Author and Jungian analyst Robert Johnson calls the religious function an inborn demand for meaning and inner experience. Theologian Paul Tillich asked us to look where you experience *depth* in your life—that's where you know God and God knows you. Carl Jung wrote simply that a religious person is one whose life has been changed by an encounter with the numinous. He added that God was the name for all things which altered his path, changed his life for better or worse. Some of those encounters and alterations will be recorded on your Soul Maps. Especially look for the incidents where enlargement is at work, where you can feel something pulling you into a larger sense of who you are.

A WINK AND A NOD

THIS GRAND and mysterious word—"numinous"—used to describe encounters with the holy, actually comes from the verb "numen": to nod or wink. This is a great, down-to-earth word to use to scan your Soul Maps:

Where do you feel the numinous . . . as a wink or nod of God?

Where is the world winking at you? How has this happened in the past? If a wink is a nod of encouragement from even an unexpected source, where do you see that on your maps?

Julia Cameron, creativity expert and author of *The Artist's Way*, once said, "We are constantly being helped, and what we are afraid of . . . is knowing that." How do your maps show you being helped over the years?

WHERE IS SURPRISE?

LOOK AT your summary pages and overall map for sheer surprise. The things in the past that surprised you, aspects of the present that are unexpected and, especially, new things that have come up that you desire for the future.

There's a method of Bible study called *lectio divina* that asks you to see what word "lights up" for you on a given day; the same question applies to your maps: What lights up, especially if it's out of left field? It's hard to hear things that are not part of our ego's construct; that's why surprise in Soul Mapping is so important. The "religious" function in us is not one that can be contained or controlled;

you can see this in the way you did not predict or "control" what came out of the exercises in this book.

Try this search for surprise using your results. Looking over all your answers and summary pages, what did you *least expect* that came up in your answers? What most surprised you?

What new ideas, different reference points, wild ways of thinking made themselves known?

TECHNIQUES FOR READING YOUR MAP

YOU CAN apply the following techniques to the whole of your assembled map, or to various parts of it, i.e., certain chapters that clump together or form sections next to each other.

THE FEEDBACK STARTS WITH YOU

THERE WILL be different energy for you in different parts of the map—not all chapters will be "high points," and that's okay, even useful. The Soul Mapping chapters help you naturally hone in on where the energy for you is—and the resistance. Knowing where you had the most bursts of creativity is important and helpful. Knowing what exercises you didn't want to do is also helpful.

- Look at your exercises and circle pages. Find the places where you wrote a lot, where the most energy is.
- Which chapters did you hate, or not want to do, or not have room for? Which did you avoid?
- Which chapter is "all about you?" Which is the one that seems particularly important or emblematic?

THE OVERALL PATTERNS AND THEMES

AS YOU look at your circles, do you notice any patterns? Between, for example, childhood desires and hidden desires today; between envy and your vision of your future, and so on.

Clarissa Pinkola Estes writes of "The river beneath the river." What overall words or themes arise from underneath your map? All of us are living certain patterns, and Soul Mapping helps us find out what they are. What are the common threads from your answers?

What threads or connective experiences do you see in your map as a whole? They can be subtle.

A friend once described hearing a piece of music that sounded like many instruments all together to him. The music teacher played it again, and traced the oboe line for him. After that, he could hear the oboe as a separate sound—it was there all along.

What "lines" can you trace in your map that were "there all along?" It can be helpful to have a trusted friend come look at your map, and help you trace, just as the music teacher helped our friend distinguish parts that were blended together. This is also something you can do for someone else who has done a Soul Map.

Short story writer Pam Houston, author of *Cowboys Are My Weakness*, spoke about her approach to creativity as "Finding the stories' singular and surreptitious formula." Your maps hold similar treasures. As you look for overall themes, look for the singular and the surreptitious.

Finally, ask yourself if and how any of the patterns are ready to take you in new directions.

YOUR MAJOR IMAGES: LEADING A SYMBOLIC LIFE

SCAN YOUR map for major images, whether in words, pictures, cut-outs, etc.

What are the central images in your life? Are you connecting with them on a regular basis?

Often images are the first hints of a transformation coming. The images that come from deep inside us have the power to change our lives. As author Marion Woodman has put it, "Instinct brings forth your images and you say yes!"

What images do you need to say "yes!" to? What would that entail?

CONNECTIONS AND RESONANCES

LOOKING FOR patterns asks you to look at the whole of the map. Sometimes the key connections you need to see are between various parts. As a creative process,

Soul Mapping brings together things that weren't together before. It asks you to perceive relationships and connections between formerly disparate elements.

Do any of your maps or answers or summary pages link up in surprising ways? Where is there a type of cross-fertilization of chapters? Is any action on your part suggested by these connections?

Don't assume certain odd bedfellows can't be brought together, i.e., don't assume barriers exist between one part of your Soul Map and another. For example, learning and envy can hook up, if you let them, and can produce a plan to acquire a skill you have always wanted.

WHEN THE PARTS DON'T FIT

"Authentic spirituality wants to open us to truth—whatever truth may be, wherever truth may take us. Such a spirituality does not dictate where we must go, but trusts that any path walked with integrity will take us to a place of knowledge. Such a spirituality encourages us to welcome diversity and conflict, to tolerate ambiguity, and to embrace paradox."

–Parker Palmer, *To Know As We Are Known: Education as Spiritual Journey*

PALMER GIVES excellent advice on reading your map in its entirety: Welcome diversity and conflict, tolerate ambiguity, and embrace paradox. In other words, whatever you see, let it in!

Any map will naturally have contradictions. Indeed, a Soul Map is an excellent tool for bringing conflicts out into the open. If instead of welcoming contradictions we cast them out unconsciously, we end up divided and disconnected. So a key step is to look at your map and not cast out but identify:

- What things just *don't fit?*
- What exercise answers do you most fiercely resist? Why? What is the source of the discomfort?

- For the parts that contradict each other, ponder them. Is there some hidden wholeness that underlies each part? Something they have in common? What do disparate parts of your self have to say to one another?

Depth psychology points out that our deepest, truest self manifests when things don't fit. Like the parables of Jesus, manifestations of the self can stand logic on its ear while revealing a deep wisdom. The self is often in the business of breaking us out of patterns that keep us too small, and your Soul Map can be an expression of that self.

DON'T GLOM ONTO ONE MEANING

EVEN WHEN we stay with a contradiction and wrestle with it, resisting the urge to dismiss it, a danger lurks that we will seize on a single, particular meaning as *the* resolution to this tangle of opposing Soul Map data. Often that resolution is indeed a gem, a glimpse of new awareness. Then we make it rigid, when it needs to stay permeable and open to additional insight. Don't stop when one meaning asserts itself; stay open to additional insight.

One way to stay open is to take some of the answers on your map—contradictory or otherwise—and brainstorm them further:

THE NON-LITERAL APPROACH.

Soul Mapping clues are as much about metaphor as literal fact. So don't disregard something—visiting Nepal, envying brain surgeons, wanting to be an astronaut, etc.—because it isn't realistic or practical. Journal about what these desires mean for you on a *symbolic* level—is there some way to incorporate them into your life now?

GENERATING ASSOCIATIONS.

You can expand the meaning of your Soul Map words and symbols by writing down all your associations with a particular item. One client, for example, had the ocean come up as both a potent image, a happy childhood memory, and a hoped-for part of her future. So she took the word "ocean" and just ran with it:

Ocean . . . summer . . . freedom . . . solitude . . . walking . . . at the edge . . . limitless possibility . . . rest . . . warmth. . . . at one . . . prayer . . . essay writing . . . inner time . . . sabbatical . . . essential.

Like ongoing maps, these associations spiral out from one small piece of one part of the Soul Map. As you extend your observations, look for one that really "clicks" or gets to the heart of the matter. For this client, it was the realization that rest and sabbatical were essential at this time, knowledge she had been resisting. The word "ocean" led her back to what she needed to hear.

SEARCHING FOR THE SHADOW

SOUL MAPS can also reveal what we have been concealing. As an overall "reading the whole map" exercise, look for the "shadow" parts of yourself. What chapters do they crop up in? Some clues about what to look for:

- What in your map do you want to keep hidden? What parts do you want to filter out, pretend aren't there, etc.?
- Where in your life are you "sneaking"—doing things out of sight or around the assumptions of others?
- Look for the gold. Where on your map do you project onto someone else energy and ability that really belong to you? Where is your self-image too small?

> "Sometimes the shadow has tremendous positive strengths that the ego
>
> won't claim because it would mean either too much responsibility or a
>
> shattering alteration of one's puny self-image."
>
> —Robert Johnson, *Inner Work*

READING YOUR MAP FOR WHERE TO GO TO WORK

AS YOU look at the parts of your map together, receiving it, contradictions and all, action may start to suggest itself. Gleefully or subtly, your Soul Map pinpoints where you need to do some work: You can see what's on fire for you, what's dying, what's been neglected that needs attention, what needs to change, where the hunger is. In this way it's a type of diagnostic tool.

The following exercises will serve as a bridge into the final chapter, "From Your Map to Movement." They are energy locators that ask you to look at the big picture of your assembled map.

NAME THE DESIRES.

Search the completed exercises for indications of changes you may want to make in your life. Pay special attention to the exercises that looked toward the future and changes known and unknown; feared and welcomed. Try to consolidate these desires; which are priorities?

WHERE ARE YOU PUSHED AND PRODDED?

Where are you being pushed and prodded by your Soul Map? If you read the existence of your many selves as a call to honor them, where are they pushing you? What new territory can you see beckoning?

If your map is a story of *process*, of change over time, of a very big picture indeed, how do you want to enhance your own process at this time? Is there a direction you need to move in? Are there people you need to meet, books you need to read, courses you need to take, places you need to go, time you need alone, etc.?

ACKNOWLEDGE THE COMMUNITIES.

As you look at the trajectory of your life, what communities or people have carried you from one transition to another? Where were you supported? Are you involved in supportive communities now? They will be an important part of any plan to implement Soul Map results.

READ YOUR CROSSROADS MOMENTS.

Look at your map for moments in your life that were real "crossroads." When tensions could no longer hold; decisions were made; something new happened; you went down a particular path. If your new Soul Map calls you to change in any way, how you handled crossroads in the past is of pivotal importance.

How did you make past decisions? What or who do you listen to?

What can you do for yourself now to create an environment supportive of transition?

WHAT DO YOU NEED TO UN-LEARN?

A classic Zen story finds an eager pupil coming for an audience with a Zen master. Before speaking, the master serves the pupil tea, by pouring . . . and pouring . . . so that first the cup is filled, then the saucer, then it spills onto the pupil's pants. He jumps up in anger and confusion. The Zen master says: "See . . . you are just like that cup. You are so full that there is no room to learn anything new. You must be emptied before we can begin."

A Zen koan reminds us: "What you have become is now your biggest obstacle." As you look at your map, especially in the patterns and themes of the past and present sections, what might you need to empty yourself of, or diminish? What is getting in your way? Are there any attitudes, assumptions, views of yourself you have outgrown but that still linger? What do you need to undo, take down, or dismantle?

THE ROADS NOT TAKEN AND REGRETTED.

An important way to read your map in its entirety is to look for places of self-betrayal. This sounds harsh, but it's not meant to. In order to go forward, we need to acknowledge the ways we hid from ourselves in the past, and what the consequences of that hiding were.

Soul Mapping is an *uncovering* exercise, and it can uncover hiding places: decisions that somehow didn't honor our instincts. Do you see any of these on your map? Paths you knew you should have taken at the time? Can you incorporate any of them now? Perhaps in new ways?

WHERE IS VOCATION LURKING?

Where on your map do you see *capacities*—things you do well and enjoy? Soul Maps are excellent devices in career counseling. They pinpoint energies that can be harnessed vocationally or avocationally. As Abraham Maslow pointed out,

"Capacities clamor to be used, and cease their clamor only when they are well used. That is, capacities are also needs."

Where on your map are there real capacities that are clamoring for expression? This expression could be in paid or volunteer work.

WHAT DOES YOUR HOUSE LOOK LIKE?

Soul Mapping is a pictorial view of the psyche—what matters, what's happened, what's emerging, what's persevering. Like the psyche, your Soul Map has many selves, many centers of consciousness. Clarissa Pinkola Estes compares this multiplicity to a New Mexican house:

> "Like the pueblos and casitas in New Mexico, the psyche is always in at
>
> least three stages—the old fallen down part, the part you live in, and the
>
> part under construction. It is like that."

> *—Women Who Run with the Wolves*

Look at all the circles of your Soul Map. What "part" or chapters or themes or tensions are you "living in?" What is the old fallen down part that maybe you have moved out of? Have you really moved, or do you still linger there? Finally, what is the part of your map that is excitedly "under construction" or that wants to be?

ENGAGE THE SAFEKEEPING SELF

The last three chapters of this book—on fear, reading your map whole, and moving with it into your life—all engage the places change is afoot. Whether your reaction to seeing shifts you need to make is fear, excitement, or deep ambivalence, a Soul Map is about movement—past, present and future.

As you move into the next chapter, keep an ear out for the sounds of what one researcher has called "the safekeeping self." It's the necessary part of ourselves that is suspicious of the new. It's protective, careful, thoughtful, and keeps you from stepping into traffic when the light is red. It also wakes up with a vengeance when it senses you might actually make a change or do something differently. Suddenly, it's not sure it's totally in charge. So it speaks, often very persuasively:

"What makes you think you can . . . ?

"You've never tried that before."

"What if you fail?"

"You're not sufficiently ___ to do that."

"This may not even work, so why try? It's too much trouble."

"You won't be good enough at it."

An important component of reading your map whole is listening for these well-reasoned objections and seeing where they crop up. We can so quickly slip into a negative view of our own leadership. Watch your self-talk with regards to your Soul Map.

Watching your self-talk does not mean trying to rid yourself of the safekeeping self; then it just goes underground and pops us in self-defeating ways. NINA: "I counsel clients that the key is to listen to what it has to say, and then remind it there is also room at the table for whatever new direction you want to try on. It's important to realize that the new Soul Map *can* co-exist with the old views. It's not either/or. Integration is possible. The safekeeping self needs to learn it's not a monopoly."

WHAT ARE YOU REALLY UP TO?

"There are only two ways to live your life. One is as though nothing is a

miracle. The other is as though everything is a miracle."

—Albert Einstein

BEFORE YOU move into the last chapter, step back, breathe deeply, and look at your answers to this chapter's exercises, and at your map in general. If Einstein was right, then one way to read your map is as though everything is a miracle.

Your map is also an evolving snapshot and by no means the "final word." You can continue to add to it and continue to "read" it. You can do new ones, especially in times of transition.

But as you pause and look at this particular one, step back and ask yourself:

"WHAT AM I REALLY UP TO HERE?"

THE DEEP self that can emerge from a Soul Map can have a different view than our usual ego view. What is your map "up to?" Marie Louise von Franz has written that "The move toward wholeness is the most ruthless of our instincts." Where do you see that move in your map? What is your self trying to bring about, either subtly or overtly? Can you call upon that ruthlessness in creative, non-destructive ways?

FOR ALL THE SECTIONS OF YOUR SOUL MAP, THE REAL QUESTIONS ARE:

1. What are you *not* doing now that you would like to be doing?
2. How are you being called into a larger sense of self?
3. What are you needing to say "no" to ? What is the "yes" that these "nos" will make room for?

Spend some time with the exercises in this chapter. Spend time reading your map. Like any rich, complex work, your map will reveal itself to you over time.

Keep coming back to it, listening to it. Then use the next chapter and the "Resources for the Journey" section to move from map into mission.

"Tell me, what is it you plan to do

with your one wild and precious life?"

–Mary Oliver, last lines of the poem "The Summer Day"

13

FROM YOUR MAP TO MOVEMENT
GOING FORTH INTO THE TERRITORY
THAT IS YOURS ALONE

"The question of whether we are moving toward death or new life is the

central question in most religious traditions."

—Parker Palmer, "Threatened with Resurrection" chapter of ***The Active Life***

"All real daring begins within."

—Eudora Welty

GROWING YOUR WINGS . . . OWNING YOUR MAPS

IN THE previous chapter, you read your maps for possible new directions, choices and longings. The natural next question is: How to put these into practice?

Soul Mapping is about authenticity: How to locate your vital energy and desire, release it onto the page and into consciousness, and then concretize it. The final step is to own that soul energy and manifest it in your life. Of course, not all Soul Map responses are the stuff of change; many are simply—and wonderfully—glimpses of your many aspects, your many selves. But as you look over your responses to the "Reading Your Map Whole" exercises, there will be specific things in your heart that aren't just descriptive, but also things you want to do, shift, or invite.

For those things, Soul Mapping asks you to move into conscious appropria-tion. With its travels into your past, Soul Mapping is about locating the roots of your maps, but it also helps you grow to soar into the future territory that is yours alone.

LIVING WITH YOUR MAPS

BEFORE ANY movement arises, the maps you created simply ask you to *live* with them. Think of them as physical companions; they hold things that can change or expand your life, so stay in touch with them.

Just as the last chapter asked you to *receive* all that is in your maps, movement asks you to *participate* with them. How will you dance with your Soul Map? Celebrate it? Explore further? Honor and amplify the contents? Will you expand the "house" where you live? What rejected stones might become the "corner-stones" of the next phase of your life?

Individuation—becoming your true self over time—has been described as moving away from an autopilot psychic life. Soul Mapping also moves you away from autopilot, since it asks you to listen deeply to what is truly yours. But listen-ing is only the first step. Again, the root of the word "hear" is the same as the root for the word "obey." There is a tough-minded two-step process implied here: that real listening will consist of hearing what you need to hear, but also moving your feet. *You* need to take the action; obey the call of what you hear. Without the action, what you hear is merely "interesting."

BRINGING ACTION INTO THE PICTURE

"Awe is what moves us forward."

—Joseph Campbell

Soul Mapping begins by dropping you into the unconscious through a wide range of journaling exercises. Various feelings may have come up for you: frustrations, hopes, desires, surprises. You may associate images and colors with some of those feelings. "Reading" your maps in the ways outlined previously helps you under-stand what the maps are saying. Action is the next step in the process.

The Soul Mapping process asks you to truly *see* what you have brought to the surface, embrace it, and act on it. Yet we realize that authentic action doesn't just arise by itself, even if you know what it may look like in a given situation. So this chapter will offer a variety of ways to invite, invoke and encourage action.

First, how do you do beginnings?

THROUGHOUT THIS book we've mentioned our belief that Soul Mapping is about *continuous annunciation*—hearing the unexpected direction; tracing the hand of God; acknowledging the angel knocking at your door. Some of those annunciations will call you into *initiation*. Soul Mapping is not a call to mindless change, but occasionally the call to begin, to initiate, is explicit.

We are all beginners throughout our lives. Soul Mapping asks you: What beginnings need to happen now? As a way to locate current urges for beginnings, ask yourself, what are the things you can't *not* do at this time in your life?

How have you done beginnings in the past? Do you think of yourself as a "beginner?" Or do you wait for others to initiate change that affects you? The word "beginner" works two ways: It describes someone who initiates, as well as someone who cultivates what Zen practice calls beginner's mind—the ability to come at something new open-minded, excited, not expert, maybe even a little fearful.

The poet David Whyte speaks about how one of the great disciplines in life is simply to come out of hiding—so that the world can find you. Where would coming out of hiding be a beginning for you?

And, as you go through your Soul Map looking for the places beginnings lurk, the attendant endings are part of the picture. We are constantly cycling between states of crucifixion (something dying, often painfully) and resurrection (something new and unexpected arising). It's tempting to avoid the dying part, but in doing so, we stifle the possible beginning.

NINA: A good friend and colleague once led a group of us on an experiential type of Scripture study. We were looking at the brief lines in the Bible on Jesus leaving Nazareth, his home town, as it were, in order to begin his ministry. We read the text, commented on it in the group, and were then asked to go to the art materials in the room and spend some time drawing *our* Nazareths. How was this story a story in our own lives? One person asked for further clarification: what did the leader mean by "our Nazareths?" The leader paused and said, "Nazareth is the place that has made you everything you are today. . . . *and* . . . keeps you from becoming everything you need to become."

What is the place . . . or person . . . or thing . . . or belief . . . that is the crux of the matter for you? That you owe so much to, *and* at the same time, holds you back? Look here for the beginnings—and the endings—your Soul Map is asking you to engage. And don't be surprised if there is a struggle. Author Marjory Bankson compares that struggle to crossing the "Poison River," which is the barrier between belief and action, the struggle between trust and fear, between "private revelation and public accountability."

———— &w ————

HOW TO GO FORWARD?
Tips and techniques

YOU HAVE identified some beginnings, fears, questions, resolutions and doubts. The desire for movement is there, and the "Poison River" flows, too. Here are some things that can take you across that river.

CONTINUE TO TALK TO YOUR MANY SELVES

"From Your Map to Movement" does not mean jettisoning your current life and running off. Movement is not about acting out, but about *incorporating* what the various parts of yourself are clamoring for. This means engaging them in dialogue, doing further mapping exercises, seeing where the tensions are, and assessing appropriate action. Based on dialogue, it's a thoughtful, not an abrupt process.

WHERE DO YOU NEED TO FEED YOURSELF?

Soul Mapping invites us to nourish the starved parts of our lives: The childhood pleasures forgotten, the current hobbies ignored, the future hopes postponed. We often thwart our own interiority, not to mention our ability to move decisively, by not feeding the parts of ourselves that in turn will truly nourish and empower us.

Where is the fire of your life? Are you encouraging it or putting it out? Where is the change energy for you? Are you nurturing it? What is calming and restorative for you? How can you do more of it?

"Feeding" these parts can be as simple as time apart, in silence, to rest, listen and re-group. One client likened it to going into a cave of her own in a time of stress—a place she could be safe, alone, and able to listen deeply. Find the particular well you need to drink from and go there; in its springs lie the inspiration to move forward.

WHAT MISSION ARE YOU ON?

There is no small "call" into movement; even small steps we take are large indeed from a spiritual perspective. But sometimes a Soul Map suggests a literal call into mission, which can be paid or volunteer, vocation or avocation.

Looking at your map, what "mission" are you on? What words describe the things you most care about? What sense of purpose floats up? What is the *difference* you are called to make? What is it that the world needs that won't get done if you don't do it? How does the world, even in a small way, need you to move forward with the contents of your map?

Seeing your map from a perspective this large can be a real impetus to movement.

MOVING THE FEET . . . TAPPING THE SHEER ENERGY OF ACTION

> "We have to recognize though that the mere fact of continuously writing entries, as is done in the keeping of a diary, is not sufficient in itself to bring about deep changes in a person's life. To achieve a significant transformation in a personality, strong forces must be generated."
>
> —Ira Progoff, *At a Journal Workshop*

Soul Mapping is an elaborate journaling process. It's powerful, revealing, hopefully fun, but to generate movement and change—the "strong forces" Progoff writes of—Soul Mapping needs you to move the feet, however slightly.

Small steps help you build and sustain momentum. They get you away from the abstract level by sending a message to your body that you're serious and engaged. James Joyce described a character in one of his novels as living "a short distance from his body." There is always a danger you will live "a short distance" from your Soul Map longings, safely removed. Soul Mapping needs to be an *embodied* technique, both in the initial drawing and brainstorming, and in the appropriation of the contents. Here are some ways to do that:

LOOK FOR SYMBOLIC INTERPRETATIONS

As we have pointed out in other chapters, it's vital you look at your Soul Map results symbolically as well as literally. Yes, writing about huge dissatisfaction with your current job in the "Today" chapter may mean you need to actually change jobs. But feeling a huge attraction to an exotic land does not mean you are supposed to move there. Envying another person's life does not mean copying it. However, aspects of the longed-for land may need to be incorporated into your current location, and the envied person can point you toward new sources of energy and strength for you.

INCARNATE YOUR MAPS

Whether your interpretation of your map's message is symbolic or literal, incarnating that interpretation in some way is vital. Doing so can be as simple as *walking* with it, while you ponder. Try moving the body in some way. The next level is to test and taste the new thing in some concrete way: to start a class, write that person, find and read that book, pray that prayer.

Ritual can help here. Honoring your new direction or movement symbolically is a powerful tool. Plant a symbol: burn a piece of paper, a cluster of sage leaves, a stick of insense; bury a vestige of what you want to leave behind; bring an object into the home that symbolizes your new resolve. Scan your maps for something that can come into your life physically, some potent reminder and generator.

"A highly conscious ritual sends a powerful message back to the unconscious, causing changes to take place at the deep levels where our attitudes and values originate."

–Robert Johnson, *Inner Work*

Take small steps

Beyond using ritual to usher in the new, or to mark turning points, break tasks down into the small steps, the acts that ground new resolves in reality. Appropriation of a Soul Map's call happens gradually; there's no need to bite off more than you can chew. Large goals or hopes can beckon on a Soul Map, seeming too shimmery, too impossible. Remember the safekeeping self from the last chapter? In the face of a large new goal, the safekeeping self balks, loudly, and sends up a cloud of protestations.

Respond by working backwards from your goal, taking apart the steps along the way that would get you there. Then take apart *those* steps, until you arrive at small, manageable ones.

On the other hand, you could just up the ante

Sometimes small steps is the only way to sneak up on movement you desire to make. Other times, the smallness can bog you down, and a very different alternative is called for. In her workshops, Laurie Beth Jones, author of many books, including *The Path: Creating Your Mission Statement for Work and for Life*, has participants generate lists of things they would like to do. When everyone's done, and thinking the list is appealing, but hard and maybe a little scary, she says: Now . . . make that list *ten times bolder*. In one swoop, you move outside boxes you didn't even know you were in. For one wild moment, you can feel your world and your sense of possibility expand. And the steps you need to take to get to what was on your original list can seem very possible. Not to mention the new possibilities the "bolder" list may hold.

Our shynesses are lifelong companions. A Soul Map respects them, but also rattles the cages of our hesitancies, if we let it.

How would your Soul Map sections which pertain to the future look if they were ten times bolder?

MOVE BEYOND OBJECTIONS

"Move from within. Don't move the way fear wants you to. Instead,

begin with a foolish project. Noah did."

—Rumi

Moving with your maps and incurring fear go hand in hand, which is one reason we devoted an entire chapter to fear and roadblocks. The fear the poet Rumi writes about can move you into a small place, one where doubts are rampant and no large project stands a chance. If you were to move in the opposite direction, refusing to be shrunk, and move towards a large response, what might your "foolish project" look like?

MOVE WITH INTENTIONALITY AND AUTHORITY

Any movement needs some deep-seated conviction and intentionality. This gets at the whole issue of authority: it takes authority to articulate intentionality believably. NINA remembers an incident that taught her this all too well:

"I was on vacation once at a holistic spa that had an "equine" workshop. It didn't involve riding; it did include three hours spent with a horse of our choosing, trying to raise its hoof so we could clean it, brushing various parts of the horse's coat, and encouraging it to walk around a ring. The workshop description promised to teach me a lot about myself. Sure, I thought. The leader spoke about what we were to do and then did it herself, naturally and calmly and with authority. Her horse responded instantly. This all looked very easy.

"So I approached my horse, and its eyes and ears were alert for more of me than I would have thought possible. Its wise, big body smelled hesitation. I reached for the foot, which stayed firmly planted on the ground like a massive pedestal. I said the words I was supposed to say, touched the right place, and . . . nothing. In this, and in other exercises, even I could hear the question marks at the end of my commands, the waver that was in my tone and in my body language. The horse was like a big, implacable mirror; he sensed my hesitations and reflected them right back in his refusal to move. If I wasn't sure of the importance of what I was asking him to do, why should he be interested?"

It's not just horses that can smell doubt and lack of clear conviction. The people we deal with as we go forward with the contents of our Soul Maps will be listening for our intentionality, and noting when it's absent. So will we.

Soul Mapping is very much about "author-izing your" life. "From Your Map to Movement" is about authorizing yourself to use and incarnate your Soul Map results. Which desires for movement can you be most intentional about at this point in your life? How can you cultivate that intentionality?

RESORT TO HORSE-TRADING

Even the clearest intentionality can run afoul of competing Soul Map contents. Keeping with the equine theme for a moment, consider what author Robert Johnson recommends you do when different parts of yourself disagree and there's an impasse. Try "horse-trading." This means you get in dialogue with each of the parts as a sort of mediator. For example, the part of you that has to work is at war with the part that wants a sabbatical. You need the work, but the sabbatical part is threatening to sabotage things. Listen to the part that wants rest. Find practical, concrete ways you can incorporate "Sabbath time" in your week. Promise the sabbatical part of your self you will make these changes, if it will let you do your work. Let the driven work part of you know it has to trade some time for the Sabbath side. This is the way to integrate the necessarily different parts of our maps and our selves.

Look for conflicts in your Soul Map. How could you work out a practical, realistic compromise between the various factions?

RECOGNIZE THE UNFIXABLES

A lot of movement with your maps is about types of *fixing*: seeing what's missing, overcoming objections, integrating opposites, etc. This careful listening and attendant muscle flexing is necessary and exhilarating. But some Soul Map conflicts can't be resolved, or the timing looks complicated indeed. The "unfixables" in this process need to be acknowledged, since they are rooted in mystery, not efficiency.

Passion. Illness. Loss. Recovery. Love. Grief. We don't control the timing of these events. Indeed, one of the great "unfixables" in the spiritual journey is timing. How long should movement take? Who's to say? As you work with the specific calls to change that may have come up in your maps, don't lose sight of the very nature of Soul Mapping: It's a process, not a product. And that process may defy the culture's expectations about how long things should take.

———— &po; ————

WORKING OVER TIME:
Soul Map movement as process

"MOVEMENT" HAS many different guises. Moving forward with your map's contents can be anything but linear. Here are some ways to think about how movement can happen:

DIRECTION, NOT DESTINATION

People use their Soul Maps to find alternatives and possibilities. They may need more information to determine whether an alternative is "right." Soul Mapping is about moving in a direction, not solving a problem. It's about exploration, not managing a process precisely. Moving toward something leaves room for mystery, for the goal to continue to clarify through research and further exploration.

This is similar to the Eastern concept of *Wu Wei*, which shows how things can happen naturally, not by forcing them, but by letting them work in their own way to produce results.

A LITTLE BIT AT A TIME

Author Linda Leonard once said in a talk that working with the unconscious is like this: You go into the forest, bring a little out . . . go back in . . . bring a little more out. You don't clear out the whole forest . . . you don't even pave a road! Owning your maps is like going into the forest . . . and taking on a little bit . . . then going back in for more treasure. It may mean doing more maps. Or expanding on a chapter you've done until it becomes an action plan. A little bit at a time reminds you that things simply take time.

JUST DO THE "NEXT THING"

The fact things can take time does not mean remaining in stasis. Indeed, there is a natural, instinctive way to move that taps the sheer power of a little bit at a time. Carl Jung described it as simply putting one foot in front of another; always doing the next thing that needs to be done.

Look at your "future" sections of all your maps. What are the "next things" that each chapter calls for you to do?

LEARN TO DESCEND

Movement can also use some directional assistance. Often, the best way to go forward, to get to the next place, to break out, is not to plunge forward but to stop and pause. To reach that still place inside where the fear lurks, yes, *and* the resolve, and the deep knowing.

To get to that place does not just involve silence, or praying, or community, though these are all important. At some point in the process there has to be a *descent*, a going down as deep and unique as we each are, and as terrifying. Sometimes we go deliberately; sometimes the ground opens up. Your knowledge of descent so far in your life is the seed for future movement.

How to descend? There are many practical, accessible tools to do so, and we have listed some of them below and some in the "Practices" section at the end of this chapter.

TRUST WAITING IN THE DARK

A key part of descending is the ability to wait, to just *be* with the results of your maps, contradictions and all. Think of the caterpillar, driven instinctively to create a dark space for itself while it is literally transformed.

Where are the cocoons in your life? The places where you can go to simply wait, as larger forces work with you? Sometimes it's precisely the dark places—depression, anxiety, tiredness—that we are reduced to so something new can arise.

INTEGRATE THE COMPETING ENERGIES

Waiting also means staying in the tension of competing or contradictory learnings from your Soul Maps.

Listen to the competing voices for and against movement and change. Dialogue in journal format with the resistant voices to see what gift or clue they might offer. Ignoring them doesn't work; they just pop out in unhelpful, disguised ways. Try listening to them, integrating their message, and moving *with* them instead of against them.

TRY A LITTLE REPENTANCE

We are being literal here. The word "repentance" simply means "to turn around." Sometimes movement happens when we make a 180–degree turn, steer in a new direction, or adjust our course slightly. When you turn around, and do something different, the view can shift radically.

Where are you going in the "wrong direction"? What new directions do your Soul Maps prompt?

LOVING ALL YOUR PARTS

We have written in other parts of this book about the importance of receiving all of your Soul Maps and, in effect, all of yourself. This receiving, this acceptance, helps with forward movement. It's not about passivity, but about a generous acknowledging, a gathering in. Arthur Miller stated this challenge to ourselves vividly in his play *After the Fall*: "I had the same dream each night—that I had a child, and even in the dream I saw that the child was my life; and it was an idiot, and I ran away. Until I thought, if I could kiss it . . . perhaps I could rest. And I bent to its broken face, and it was horrible . . . but I kissed it. I think one must finally take one's life in one's arms."

THE COST OF NOT MOVING

ANY CHAPTER on moving forward with the contents of your Soul Map needs to look at the topic in its entirety: The rewards of movement; how hard it is "to take one's life in one's arms"; ways to do it; how it takes time; and some of the consequences of *not* moving forward in ways you know you should. Often saying "no" is an initial response, just temporary, we tell ourselves, while we gather more data. Then the "no" becomes the status quo, and very difficult to dislodge.

While we usually fixate on the consequences of moving forward with something, it's all too easy to forget to calculate the cost of staying put, of avoiding and not receiving whatever impetus your map may be giving you. Being aware of the costs of saying "no" to your maps is an important form of stewardship. This is not just a safe church fundraising term. We are all stewards—caretakers—of our talents and dreams, and our lives are a unique response to those gifts. Soul Maps are designed to gather a lot of those gifts in one place.

Implicit in this notion of stewardship is the cost of not using the gifts we have. *The Gospel of Thomas*, a recently discovered text compiled of sayings atrributed to Jesus, states the cost bluntly: "If you bring forth what is within you, what you bring forth will save you. If you do not bring forth what is within you, what you do not bring forth will destroy you."

This harsh but ultimately liberating idea simply echoes what psychotherapy already knows: that life calls us forward, and if you don't go forward you begin to self-destruct in ways that can be obvious or subtle. That the very things that need expressing will turn on us if we do not heed them. This does not mean going forward is easy. As philosopher Søren Kierkegaard pointed out, "To venture causes anxiety, but not to venture is to lose oneself."

If we had to sum up the Soul Mapping purpose in one phrase, we would say *"to prevent loss of self."* Soul Mapping is a way to keep your dreams, fragments, plans, and hopes alive and part of your future. It's a way to *wake up* and incorporate vital things before they get lost. Kierkegaard, in his writing about various types of despair, talked about the particularly nasty type of despair that is one of defiance: knowing what you need to do to be yourself and then not doing it.

This despair can be very subtle. It can look like simple, sensible hesitation. NINA: "I remember a Vocare workshop we gave on vocational discernment, and a woman there told us her story: She knew ten years ago she should switch careers, and . . . she paused. Here she was, ten years later, very unhappy and now really having to switch.

"In my own past, I remember a life-design workshop leader I once studied with who spent four days listening to me go on about various possibilities and plans. Part of his summary of my work included the comment: "I would ask you to be a better steward of your finitude. Time is a measure of life, and you are beyond getting ready to live.

That injunction—be a better steward of my finitude—was a potent gift, reminding me of the dangers of frittering away precious time. Your Soul Maps ask you to be stewards of your life, of your time. They want to be *lived*, not hesitated over, or forgotten, or shoved in a corner. They can be either a wellspring of creativity and new life—or a repository, as in Rilke's phrase, 'repository of unlived things.' "

Yes, we all have these repositories. The question is how much is in there, and how much you need to get those lives out of their closet and try them on. Soul Mapping is the bridge that helps you be aware of, accept, and then act on all that wants to be lived. Certain practices can help with that transition.

PRACTICES THAT FEED MOVEMENT

VARIOUS SPIRITUAL practices can be extremely helpful in following your map's directions. They can help you do the "descending" to a central part of yourself that knows and trusts. They can help silence the negative voices. Look over this menu, pick the ones that appeal to you at this time, and treat them as true *practices*: to be done with regularity, even when you don't feel like it. Practices offer their gifts over time, as they become knit into the fabric of your days. And feel free to add to this list.

PRAYER AND MEDITATION

Yes, you created your Soul Map and yes, it's up to you to review it, let it in, and move with it in creative ways. But you're not alone in this process. Just as the ego can't control what came up on the map, there is a power greater than you that can help the map come about—perhaps in unexpected ways, and usually in kairos time—God's time—not in our sense of linear time. We see this grace often with clients as they shift in small, yet undeniable ways, towards some larger sense of possibility. Prayer and meditation—talking to God, listening to God—are rivers anyone can step into. You might try asking for what you need to honor in your maps; it could be strength, humor, courage, intentionality, etc.

SILENCE AND SOLITUDE

Time spent apart, alone and in the quiet, is probably the most helpful thing you can do to move forward with your maps. Community is powerful, too (see below), but hours away from family, coworkers, friends, noise and other distractions usher in powerful listening time you can trust.

WALKING

Wisdom and strength come through the feet. Are you pondering a shift suggested by your Soul Map? Walk with it, for at least thirty minutes. Literally embody it as you move forward walking. This is far more powerful—and helpfully dislodging—than always pondering your next move from a chair. Trust your senses as you walk.

JOURNALING AND RECORDING

If there is a particular part of your map that you want to work with, or a particular chapter that holds a lot for you, don't let the recording process stop with the exercises in this book. Now that you have unleashed various energies, images, symbols, and insights around a topic, thoughts will continue to come to you at various times, and they may be fleeting. Find a way that works for you to capture them for future reference.

BALANCING

Jungian analyst and author Thomas Lavin talks about how important it is for each person to find their own combination of "love, work, pray and play."

You have floated up Soul Map contents on a variety of areas. How can you read and implement them so these four areas are nourished? One of the first balancing questions is: How can you make space in your life for what is important on your maps that isn't getting space now? What jumps out at you as needing more attention?

PLEASURES: INVITE THE POWER OF POETRY, MUSIC AND ART AND MOVEMENT

In our last Soul Mapping workshop, we deliberately scheduled some segments with a body movement specialist—someone who could lead the whole room in getting out of their heads and just loosening up. Our resistance to moving forward isn't just logistical or logical; it's in the body. And the body responds to the power of dance, stretch, breathwork, poetry, art, music, and more. Feed yourself well on all these as you work with your maps.

INCLUDE YOUR "COMMUNITY OF ENCOURAGEMENT"

"Claiming" your Soul Map is an ongoing practice unto itself. Articulating it can be an important first step. In workshops, we have people speak about their map contents to each other. Something powerful and authorizing happens when you *voice* the contents, even to strangers.

As we mentioned in the "Today" chapter, David Whyte talks about the "courageous conversations" we need to have with people at any given moment. Soul Mapping is an invitation to come out of hiding, to show up for these conversations, even if you don't know where they will lead.

Looking at the results of your map, what are the "courageous conversations" you need to have and with whom?

WHO ARE YOUR SOUL MOVERS?

NINA: "A friend recently paid me the delightful, off-the-cuff compliment of saying I was a 'soul mover' for her. Not someone directive, but someone who could listen, exhort or point things out from my own place of passion, and utterly support and love her in her current struggle.

"Who are the people in your life who can help you move with the results of your map? Who are the people who see you in large, not limiting ways? Go to them, be with them, show your map to them. Invite them to do one, too. Speak to this community of encouragement of your hopes and fears. This way lies movement, support, and love.

"And think of ways you can be that soul mover for people in your life."

Note: The "Resource" section of this book lists books and tapes specially chosen to help deepen the Soul Mapping process and help you with some of the above practices.

⊷

HOW MOVEMENT IS MET

WHAT DOES it *look* and *feel* like when you start to move forward with your maps? By awakening the unconscious mind, it initiates a process of change. It starts a journey, and changes what comes to you or what you notice in mysterious ways.

As you notice more, you decide what aspects of yourself to focus on, and you can watch what you focus on grow. You learn to trust your instincts.

Jungian analyst and author Robert Johnson deftly outlines the rock-solid benefits of this work, in his book *Inner Work:* "A great sense of security develops from this process of individuation. One begins to understand that it isn't necessary to struggle to be like someone else, for by being one's own self one stands on the surest ground. We realize that to know ourselves completely and to develop all the strengths that are built into us is a lifetime task. We don't need to make an imitation of someone else's life. There is no further need for pretensions, for what is already ours is riches enough, and far more than we ever expected."

So gather up your riches from all the exercises in your arms and move forward, whether gently, boldly, doubtfully or joyfully. The ground—your Soul Map—is sure indeed.

A Final Note

"What lies before us

and what lies beyond us

is tiny compared to

what lies within us."

–Henry David Thoreau

SOUL MAPPING is about profound and playful exploration of all that lies within. It is also about coming home, perhaps for the first time, to where you truly dwell.

In some of the versions of the fairy tale "The Handless Maiden," there is a sign above the door where the heroine spends seven important years becoming who she needs to become. Fate has brought her and her child to a house in the woods that will be her sheltering place. The sign reads:

Here all dwell free.

Doing your maps and incorporating them into your life helps you get to that place where you can be free, where you can act from a center that is yours and yours alone.

The ground you are standing on—the raw detail of your maps—is holy ground. It is detailed, challenging and confirming ground. And it brings up one of the ultimate questions, according to spiritual tradition.

A familiar Hasidic story tells us that the real "judgment day" question we have to worry about is not why weren't you brave like Moses, or like anyone for that matter. The question we are supposed to fear—and embrace—is: Why weren't we ourselves? Why wasn't I NINA? Why wasn't I DICK, or KEN? What happened?

Ultimately, Soul Mapping helps you *reveal* who you're supposed to be, and gives you some ways to honor what you find. We wish you Godspeed as you go forward: Have fun, be bold, and trust.

RESOURCES FOR THE JOURNEY

THE SOUL MAPPING process invites you to listen to many parts of your life. Here are some additional resources that also reflect on some of the vital areas touched on by *Soul Mapping*. So many good books and tapes exist to support the individual journey your maps invoke; this list is deliberately small and personal—a gathering of some particularly wise and helpful guides, offered with gratitude for their gifts along the way.

VOCATION

Boldt, Laurence G. *How to Find the Work You Love*. Penguin Arkana, 1996.

Bolles, Richard. *How to Find Your Mission in Life*. 10 Speed Press, 1992.

Farnham, Suzanne G. et. al. *Listening Hearts: Discerning Call in Community*. Morehouse Publishing, 1991. Great compilation of the characteristics of call, drawn from a close study of many spiritual classics.

Hillman, James. *The Soul's Code: In Search of Character and Calling*. Random House, 1996.

Jacobsen, Mary. *Hand-me Down Dreams: How Families Influence Our Career Paths and How We Can Reclaim Them*. Harmony Books, 1999.

Jones, Laurie Beth. *The Path: Creating Your Mission Statement for Work and for Life*. Hyperion, 1996.

Levoy, Gregg: *Callings: Finding and Following an Authentic Life*. Harmony Books, 1997.

Palmer, Parker. *Let Your Life Speak: Listening for the Voice of Vocation*. Jossey Bass, 2000.

Sher, Barbara. *I Could Do Anything if I Only Knew What It Was*. Delacorte, 1994.

Whyte, David. *The Heart Aroused: Poetry and the Preservation of Soul in Corporate America*. Doubleday Currency, 1994. Would also highly recommend his tapes: you can order a list of them by calling 360-221-1324.

CHILDHOOD AND LIFE CYCLE

Erikson, Erik. *The Life Cycle Completed*. W.W. Norton, 1997.
Jung, C. G. *The Undiscovered Self*. Princeton-Bollingen, 1990.
Miller, Alice. *Prisoners of Childhood*. Basic Books, 1981.

CREATIVITY

Cameron, Julia: *The Artist's Way*. J. P. Tarcher, 1992.
Csikszentmihalyi, Mihaly. *Flow*. First Harper Perennial, 1990.
_____. *Finding Flow*. Basic Books, 1997.
Fincher, Suzanne. *Creating Mandalas for Insight, Healing and Self-Expression*. Shambhala, 1991.

WORKING WITH YOUR DREAMS

Johnson, Robert. *Inner Work: Using Dreams and Active Imagination for Personal Growth*. HarperSanFrancisco, 1986. There's an abundance of books on dreams, but this one helps you map a dream's meaning for *you* in a way no other book does.
Sanford, John. *Dreams: God's Forgotten Language*. HarperCollins, 1989.

MID-LIFE AND TRANSITIONS

Brennan, Anne, and Brewi, Janice. *Celebrate Mid-life: Jungian Archetypes and Mid-life Spirituality*. Crossroad Publishing Company, 1989.
Bridges, William. *Transitions*. Addison-Wesley, 1980. A classic. If you read only one book on change, this should be it.
Hollis, James. *The Middle Passage: From Misery to Meaning at Mid-life*. Inner City Books, 1993.

Hudson, Frederic. *LifeLaunch: A Passionate Guide to the Rest of Your Life*. The Hudson Institute, 1995. Simply one of the best overviews of adult development cycles and change. To order, call 1-800-582-4401.

Monk Kidd, Sue. *When the Heart Waits: Spiritual Direction for Life's Sacred Questions*. HarperCollins, 1990.

McClelland, Carol. *The Seasons of Change: Using Nature's Wisdom to Go Through Life's Inevitable Ups and Downs*. Conari Press, 1998.

Rupp, Joyce. *Dear Heart, Come Home: The Path of Mid-life Spirituality*. Crossroad Publishing Company, 1997.

Stein, Murray. *In Mid-life: A Jungian Perspective*. Spring Publications, 1983.

THE SHADOW AND UNKNOWN PARTS OF OURSELVES

Bly, Robert. *A Little Book on the Human Shadow*. HarperSanFrancisco, 1988.

Johnson, Robert. *Owning Your Own Shadow*. HarperSanFrancisco, 1991.

Pearson, Carol. *Awakening the Heroes Within*. HarperCollins, 1991.

Zweig, Connie. *Romancing the Shadow: A Guide to Soul Work for a Vital, Authentic Life*. Ballantine Wellspring, 1997.

RELATIONSHIPS

Hollis, James. *The Eden Project: In Search of the Magical Other*. Inner City Books, 1998. Essential reading for conscious relationships.

Keen, Sam. *The Passionate Life: Stages of Loving*. HarperCollins, 1983.

FEAR

Susan Jeffers, Susan. *Feel the Fear and Do It Anyway*. Fawcett Columbine, 1987. A wise, helpful classic.

GOING FORWARD...

Ban Breathnach, Sarah. *Something More: Excavating Your Authentic Self*. Warner Books, 1998.

Bankson, Marjory. *Call to the Soul: Six Stages of Spiritual Development*. Innisfree Press, 1999.

Caliandro, Arthur. *Simple Steps: Ten Things You Can Do to Create an Exceptional Life*. McGraw-Hill, 1999.

Dols, William L. *Awakening the Fire Within*. Superb overview of education/transformation as leading out what is already within people. To order: Call 800-624-4644. Published by The Educational Center in St. Louis, Missouri.

Dyer, Mary Heron. *Year of Jubilee: A Guidebook for Women Reinventing Their Lives*. Dandelion Seed Press, 1999.

Estes, Clarissa Pinkola. *Women Who Run with the Wolves*. Ballantine Books, 1992.

Leider, Richard J. and Shapiro, David A. *Re-Packing Your Bags: Lighten Your Load for the Rest of Your Life*. Berrett-Koehler Publishers, 1995.

Nemeth, Maria. *The Energy of Money: A Spiritual Guide to Financial and Personal Fulfillment*. Ballantine Wellspring, 1999.

Oliver, Mary. *New and Selected Poems*. Beacon Press, 1992.

Barbara Sher. *Wishcraft: How to Get What You Really Want*. Ballantine Books, 1979.

_____, *It's Only Too Late If You Don't Start Now*. Delacorte, 1998.

Sinetar, Marsha. *Elegant Choices, Healing Choices: Finding Grace and Wholeness in Everything We Choose*. Paulist Press, 1988.

O'Donohue, John: *Eternal Echoes: Exploring Our Yearning to Belong*, 1999.

Progoff, Ira: *At a Journal Workshop: Revised*. Dialogue House, 1992.

SPIRITUALITY AND PRAYER

Brussat, Frederic and Mary Ann. *Spiritual Literacy: Reading the Sacred in Everyday Life*. Scribner's, 1998.

_____, *Spiritual Rx: Prescriptions for Living a Meaningful Life*. Hyperion, 1999.

Buechner, Frederick. *Listening to Your Life: Daily Meditations*. HarperCollins, 1992.

Campbell Johnson, Ben. *Living Before God: Deepening Our Sense of the Divine Presence*. Wm. B. Eerdmans, 2000.

Edwards, Tilden. *Living in the Presence: Spiritual Exercises to Open Our Lives to the Awareness of God*. HarperCollins, 1995.

Howes, Elizabeth Boyden, Phillips, Dorothy Berkley and Nixon, Lucille, eds. *The Choice is Always Ours: The Classic Anthology on the Spiritual Way.* HarperCollins, 1975.

Nouwen, Henri J. M. *The Only Necessary Thing: Living a Prayerful Life.* Compiled and edited by Wendy Wilson Greer. Crossroad Publishing Company, 1999.

Sinetar, Marsha. *Ordinary People as Monks and Mystics.* Paulist Press, 1986.

Ulanov, Ann and Barry. *Primary Speech: A Psychology of Prayer.* John Knox Press, 1982.

The Bible Workbench. Lectionary-based readings bring the Bible to life and relate it to key questions of learning and transformation. Interactive and eye-opening. Edited by William L. Dols; published by The Educational Center. To order: Call 800-624-4644.

The Vocare Group Products and Services

If you liked some of the ideas in this book, consider continuing your journey with the products and services of the Vocare Group.

ஐ Soul Mapping Retreats

The Vocare Group can facilitate Soul Mapping retreats for your group, company or congregation. These powerful, productive gatherings can range from a couple of hours to a weekend or longer. Call 212-585-2722 for more information or send an email to VocareGrp@aol.com.

ஐ Individual consulting

The Emergent Self: Consultation Services
The Vocare Group can work with you personally on many vital areas pertaining to work: career transition, skills identification, vocational discernment, interview coaching, and much more. Call 212-585-2722 for more information or send an email to VocareGrp@aol.com.

❧ BOOKS AND AUDIO TAPES

WHERE DO I GO FROM HERE? AN INSPIRATIONAL GUIDE TO MAKING
AUTHENTIC CAREER AND LIFE CHOICES
by Dr. Kenneth Ruge. Book: $12.95. McGraw-Hill.
A personal road map to connecting with your true self and tapping the power
within you.

TAKE CONTROL OF YOUR LIFE: HOW TO CONTROL FATE, LUCK, CHAOS,
KARMA, AND LIFE'S OTHER UNRULING FORCES
by Dr. Richard Shoup. Book: $12.95. McGraw-Hill.
A fascinating, empowering 7-steps action plan to create positive momentum
in all areas of your life.

FINDING YOUR PATH: THE VOCARE WORKSHOP
2 tapes plus workbook: $29.95
If you can't get to a Vocare workshop in person, ordering this set of tapes is
the best way to go deeper in your search for your personal mission. You will
be guided through a unique process designed to uncover your true desires and
gifts, understand past influences, and help you respond to the call of new
directions. Accompanied by an interactive workbook journal.

The following tapes were recorded live at New York City's Marble Collegiate Church:

WHERE AM I GOING, GOD?
by Nina H. Frost. 2 tapes: $15.95
How can you feel God's guidance in your everyday life? In your choice of
work, in relationships, in decision making? This wide-ranging series uncovers
many clues that help you discern what you are called to do in your spiritual
journey.

WRESTLING WITH YOUR ANGEL
by Dr. Kenneth Ruge. 2 tapes: $15.95
How can you find the courage and endurance to grapple with your particular
life challenge? Here are a variety of spiritual and psychological tools to help
you take heart and wrestle with your angel.

OPPORTUNITY THINKING
by Dr. Richard Shoup. 2 tapes: $15.95
Taking the phenomena of chaos, luck, karma, and grace, Dr. Shoup looks at ways each of us can make the most out of what life gives us.

DEEPENING YOUR SPIRITUALITY
by Dr. Kenneth Ruge. 2 tapes: $15.95
An inspiring and practical discussion of ways you can go deeper in your spiritual journey, with useful suggestions on daily practices.

PRAYER: BEYOND THE FIRST STEPS
by Nina H. Frost. 2 tapes: $15.95
How can you feel God's guidance in your everyday life? In your choice of work, in relationships, in decision making? This wide-ranging series uncovers many clues that help you discern what you are called to do in your spiritual journey.

LISTEN TO YOUR DREAMS
by Dr. Kenneth Ruge. 2 tapes: $15.95
Dreams offer us a gateway to the wisdom of the unconscious mind. Unlock the meanings of your dreams and tap the power of the unconscious.

RESPONSIBILITY THINKING
by Dr. Richard Shoup. 2 tapes: $15.95
Reframing our lives in terms of personal leadership, Dr. Shoup looks at responsibility as a way to make an effective response to the challenges life brings.

MONEY, SEX, AND POWER
by Dr. Kenneth Ruge. 2 tapes: $15.95
Money, sex, and power are cultural icons which can seduce us from a true and authentic path. Dr. Ruge offers insight and spiritual leverage to help you put your life in the proper perspective.

☙ SPECIAL OFFER:

Order **Finding Your Path: The Vocare Workshop** plus any two companion tape titles listed above for a total of $49.95 plus shipping and handling (regularly $61.85).

To order any of The Vocare Group tapes, please contact Pathway Book Service. Checks, VISA and MasterCard accepted.

Phone orders: Call 800-345-6665.
Mail orders: Send to Pathway Book Service, 4 White Brook Road, Gilsum, NH 03448.
Fax orders: Fax to 603-357-2073.
E-mail orders: pbs@top.monad.net

Please make checks payable to Pathway Book Service.
For credit card orders, please provide card number and expiration date.

YOUR CIRCLE PAGE

Acknowledgments

———— ❧ ————

Books have their sources in so many places and people, and offering thanks to everything and everyone who graced a book's emergence becomes wonderfully impossible.

Soul Mapping is no exception to this dilemma of abundance. As three collaborators, colleagues and friends, we offer profound thanks to all the family and friends who have encouraged and prodded and loved us. We also want to acknowledge our clients, whose stories, faith, perseverance and humor are ongoing.

Soul Mapping is a book about the spirit of *inquiry*: a willingness to look beneath the surface; to struggle toward consciousness; to examine, accept, and even celebrate all the parts of ourselves. This work needs community, and both as The Vocare Group and as individuals we have been blessed with communities and mentors who do not shrink from the tensions and paradoxes any real inquiry produces.

Education—*Educare*—means to "lead out of" and certain people and places deserve special mention for helping us pull out of ourselves what needed expression:

❧ Marble Collegiate Church in New York City, where the Revs. Arthur Caliandro, Florence Pert, Robert Williams, and Kimberleigh Jordan have encouraged us with many teaching opportunities.

❧ Dr. David Kelly of Kenwood Psychological Services, who also provided us with opportunities for growth and service.

❧ The Guild for Psychological Studies and Four Springs Seminars in California, where Elizabeth Boyden Howes and others change lives by helping people link their story to the larger biblical Story.

Journey into Wholeness conferences in North Carolina, for being church in the best sense of the word, and a place that integrates Jungian psychology with Christian spirituality so compellingly.

As principal author of this book, Nina would like to add:

Love and thanks to my parents and sisters, for the many ways they embrace and encourage. I would also like to thank the Revs. Mark S. Anschutz, Thomas Cushman, and Mary Cushman formely of St. James' Episcopal Church in New York City, for being true teachers, pastors and friends—ever able with the ineffable and the demands of becoming a new creation. A special thanks to the Rev. William Dols, for his friendship, leadership, and sheer ability to make ambiguity and wilderness places of transformation. He is a true teacher.

Others were vital in moving this book from vision to reality:

A particularly fervent thanks to our editor, Matthew Lore of Marlowe & Company, whose astuteness, creativity, and on-target standards helped lead us to a finished manuscript; and to our agent Gareth Esersky of Carol Mann Agency, for energy, savvy and friendship. Barry Lenson, cohort and scribe, added his invaluable touch to some chapters; Nicole Walker and Lesley McBain were the expert copy-editors; and Pauline Neuwirth created the clear, graceful design.

Various books and workshops, crises and homecomings, and deaths and resurrections all contributed . . . and continue to do so. Kate (Ça), Sharon, and Patty . . . thank you for your essential, life-giving friendship and counsel. And, a note of ongoing, still-surprised gratitude, celebration, and love to Robert, who brings so much into being.

Finally, thanks be to God.

About the Authors

THE VOCARE GROUP was formed by three colleagues to apply the tools, practices, and ideas of spirituality to the challenges posed by the career and personal transitions we face throughout our lives. They conduct workshops together and are each available for individual consultations with clients. A list of their other books and tapes is located in the *Resources for the Journey* section of this book. They can be reached via their web site, www.vocare.com, or by calling 212-585-2722.

KENNETH C. RUGE   NINA H. FROST   RICHARD W. SHOUP

NINA H. FROST is a vocational counselor and spiritual director in private practice in New York City. She works with individuals who want to explore the issues of career discernment, right livelihood, and transition. She also designs and leads retreats and workshops that help people integrate spirituality with the challenges posed by career and personal transitions. Past positions include president of The Corporate Word, Inc., a communications consulting firm. She is the author of *Successful Model Letters for Executives* (Weka Publishing).

KENNETH. C. RUGE, D. MIN., is a New York City–based psychotherapist, motivational speaker, and adjunct minister at Norman Vincent Peale's Marble Collegiate Church. Dr. Ruge has over 20 years of experience working with clients in search of new meaning and direction in their lives. He is also a popular workshop leader and the author of Where *Do I Go From Here? An Inspirational Guide to Making Authentic Career and Life Choices* (McGraw-Hill, 1998).

RICHARD. W. SHOUP, D. MIN., is a Presbyterian minister, psychotherapist, consultant and Director of Consultative Services at the Blanton-Peale Institute. He has worked for over 15 years with individuals struggling with work and other life issues. He is a recognized authority on bringing a new perspective to career transitions, human relationships, and life change, and the author of *Take Control of Your Life: How to Control Fate, Luck, Chaos, Karma, and Life's Other Unruly Forces* (McGraw-Hill, 2000).